WOODEN CLOCK CASES

David Bryant

STACKPOLE
BOOKS

Copyright © 1994 by David Bryant

Published in 1995 by
STACKPOLE BOOKS
5067 Ritter Road
Mechanicsburg, PA 17055

Printed in England

First Edition

10 9 8 7 6 5 4 3 2 1

Library of Congress Cataloging-in-Publication Data
Bryant, David, 1941–
    Wooden clock cases / David Bryant. — 1st ed.
      p. cm.
    Includes index.
    ISBN 0-8117-2597-9 (pbk.)
    1. Woodwork—Patterns. 2. Clocks and watches—Design and construction. I. Title.
TT200.B79 1995
684.1'6—dc20

94-46442
CIP

Contents

To my Father

Acknowledgements

I would like to express my sincere thanks to all those who offered help and guidance in the preparation of this book. I am particularly in debt to the following museums, country houses, and clock dealers who allowed me to measure up the clocks featured herein: Lyme Park, National Trust, for the Daniel Quare bracket clock (Chapter 2) and the marquetry longcase clock (Chapter 15); Terry Lees, Derbyshire Clocks, for the arch dial bracket clock (Chapter 3) and the tavern clock (Chapter 11); Max Uppink, Cranford Clocks, for the balloon clock (Chapter 6), the Vienna regulator (Chapter 9) and the Black Forest wall clock (Chapter 13); Gerard Campbell, Maple House, Lechlade for the nine-light Viennese regulator (Chapter 8); Roy Clements, Coppelia Clocks, Plumley for the London pagoda longcase clock (Chapter 17); and Roman and Maz Piekarski, Tabley Cuckoo Clock Museum, for the cuckoo clock (Chapter 14). For the remaining clocks I am in debt to many friends and members of the Antiquarian Horological Society who kindly allowed me access to measure their cases.

I owe especial thanks to Peter Torry for checking the manuscript and offering me much advice and words of wisdom on horological matters, and to Mr R. Shepherd for the jacket photograph. Finally my thanks go to my wife and family who supported me with extraordinary patience whilst I was working on this project and who finally called 'time'.

Preface

The original idea of a book of period clock case designs came out of a realization that there were few, if any, available. While designs do exist many seemed to me to be what I would describe as pseudo period clocks having features of antique clocks but also influenced by modern design, a combination which somehow does not ring true. In these circumstances I decided to make a thorough investigation of clock case design and construction. At the beginning I thought that it would be difficult to find more than 15 representative cases, but as I delved further into horological casework I found an incredible variety, to the extent that at the end I was having politely to decline offers of help. Among those offering assistance were country houses, horological museums, antique dealers, collectors and private individuals.

In all, 21 different clock case designs are presented, broadly falling into three categories: table clocks (i.e. bracket clocks), wall mounted clocks and floor standing clocks (i.e. longcase). There are a good range of English bracket clock designs including arch dial, balloon, broken arch and lancet style cases, and also a very early Daniel Quare dome top bracket clock. Under the wall clock section there are designs for two English dial clocks including a rare yet simple black dial case. I have also included a chapter on tavern clock design which I hope will make interesting reading. With regard to English longcase clocks there are four designs including an early marquetry case with a rising hood; a classic London pagoda; and two attractive country style longcases, one having a swan neck pediment and the other a Lancashire case with a caddy top. Continental designs are catered for in the form of a couple of Vienna regulators, a cuckoo clock, and a Black Forest wall clock.

Every clock is measured from a period original and in some instances these are of provenanced origin. In the design drawings I have preserved as far as possible the original dimensions, but where a change has been made this is highlighted for those interested in the historical aspect.

The designs are suited to all tastes and all ranges of ability. For example, the black dial and tavern clocks have no complex bezels to fit and only require woodturning and joinery skills. At the other end of the scale the marquetry and pagoda longcase clocks may test one's ability, but just because a clock looks impressive and has more components does not mean to say it is that much more difficult to build. One interesting fact to come out of my review of clock case design is that unlike furniture which uses all sorts of jointing, clocks are almost entirely constructed of simple half joints and there is hardly a mortice and tenon or dovetail to be seen. If there are any special problems I think it has to be in the production of the mouldings which do require some knowledge of routing. In the end it really all boils down to the acquired skills, and there is always room to learn a new one.

The book commences with an introductory chapter on basic horology concerning movements, escapements, strikes and chimes, and general horological terminology. I included this as a useful background particularly for those who are approaching the subject with a woodworking rather than a horological background. In general each design is prefaced with notes on the history and evolution of the particular case style, and I have presented them chronologically as far as it was possible. I have assumed that the reader has acquired the basic skills of joinery, woodturning, marquetry etc., which are adequately covered in other specialist books. The text is therefore limited to a suggested order of assembly, and additional notes that may not be clear from the drawings. However, I have taken trouble to amplify specialized aspects such as making split turnings and ebonizing. The design drawings are in sufficient detail for the reader to be able to make a facsimile reproduction. Metric dimensions have been adopted, this being the accepted European standard today, and are generally much easier to read than imperial measurements. A metric/imperial conversion table is included at the back of the book for those interested.

One of the difficulties I recognized in presenting a design book of period clock cases is that of marrying a movement to the case. I considered the idea of recommending particular movements to suit each individual case, but finally decided the reader should be given freedom of choice, and a list of suppliers is given in the appendix. For most designs you should be able to procure dials, bezels and movements to suit each case, but to cover the possibility that there still might be difficulties, where casework

adaption is necessary I have indicated the key dimensions to adjust. In some instances I know that problems will arise here and there: for example the tavern clock design which should ideally be fitted with a movement having a seconds pendulum, where these are made principally for longcase clocks. Also where cuckoo clocks were concerned I found the supply of movement components relatively easy to come by, but obtaining a complete movement of any quality was more difficult. In special cases I have been obliged to name a supplier because I knew of no other. In these and other situations I have endeavoured to offer constructive solutions so that one way or another you will hopefully succeed in your chosen project.

Finally I hope that this book will prove an inspiration to all those interested in making clock cases. If you want to learn more on clock casework or matters generally related to horology, then I would unhesitatingly recommend that you join one of the societies listed in the appendix. Here you find new friends and a band of people dedicated to an exchange of views on this subject, and before long you will find yourself hooked on the subject like I am.

CHAPTER 1

The measurement of time

For anyone contemplating making clock cases, a basic understanding of the measurement of time, clock movements, escapements, strikes and chimes is useful and indeed desirable. For many this may be common knowledge, but for others perhaps approaching the subject of clock case construction through an interest in woodwork rather than horology, this may be unfamiliar ground. In this introductory chapter, therefore, I propose to briefly discuss these aspects and the horological terminology used, so that when the reader is confronted with words such as anchor, dead beat and motion work in the designs which follow, this will be fully appreciated. Let us start by looking briefly at the history of time.

Early clocks

The earliest known method used for measuring time is the sundial. This was based on the principle of the moving shadow cast by the sun, and there is evidence to suggest that the Chinese were developing sundials as early as 400BC or even before this. This very simple astronomical device consists of an angular post or gnomon set into a circular board marked with hours around the perimeter. As the sun moves across the sky the position of the shadow cast by the gnomon changes, from which the time of day is estimated. For a sundial with a horizontal board the angle of the gnomon is made parallel to the earth's axis. Although sundials are traditionally set horizontal they do not have to be so, and are often seen on the sides of buildings (Fig 1.1). Their basic limitation is that they can only measure the daytime hours, providing of course that the sun is shining.

Other early methods used to measure time

1.1 *Sun dial*

were water clocks, sand glasses and candle clocks. Water clocks such as clepsydra of Byzantium and European origin worked on the principle of the fluid leaking from a container at

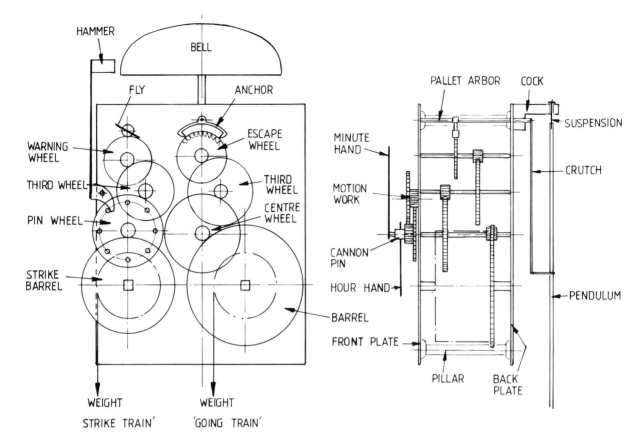

1.2 *Typical movement*

a controlled rate through a small hole, and the arrangement was often connected to a mechanical float. Early sand glasses were generally made in two pieces joined at the centre and date from about the fourteenth century onwards. The candle clock registers time by the wax gradually burning down through a row of marked graduations, and also has the benefit of providing light at night. The mechanical movement fitted with a gear train as we know it today is a relatively modern innovation, dating from roughly 1400 AD onwards.

Movements, pendulums and escapements

A typical movement for a mechanical clock powered either by a coil spring or a weight system is illustrated in Fig 1.2. It consists of a pair of brass plates between which is mounted a gear train which drives the hands pointing to the hour on the dial plate mounted at the front. In horological terms the mechanism of gears and pinions driving the hands is known as the 'going train', and that which makes the clock strike the hour is called the 'strike train'. Outside the front plate is the 'motion work' which is the 12:1 reduction gearing used to drive the hour hand slower than the minute hand.

To stop the movement from rapidly unwinding an 'escapement' is fitted to slow this down and release the motion in incremental steps. To control the rate at which it does this, either a 'balance wheel' or a 'pendulum' is fitted. The earliest mechanical clocks were regulated by means of a balance wheel or foliot. The invention of the pendulum in 1657 is generally attributed to Christian Huygens, but it was Ahasuerus Fromanteel who first incorporated it commercially into clock movements in 1658. The pendulum quickly established itself as an extremely reliable method of regulating a clock and it is largely to contain this and the movement above that clock cases have evolved.

Up until recently the balance wheel was generally used in watches though it has been superseded to some degree by electronic regulators e.g. quartz and microchips, but the pendulum is still used on clocks. The period of oscillation of a pendulum is dependent on gravity and the length between the suspension

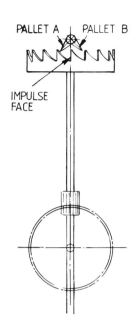

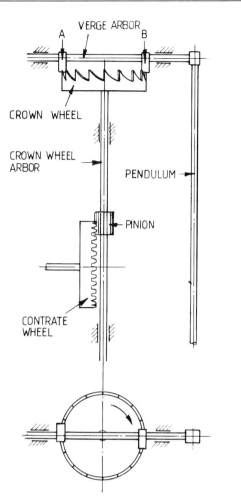

1.3 (Above & Right) *Verge escapement*

point and the centre of mass of the bob. For those interested the formula is given in the appendix on pendulum vibration. The clock case designs in this book are principally for movements fitted with pendulum regulation. There are three common forms of escapement: the verge, the anchor and the deadbeat which I will now discuss.

Verge escapement

The verge escapement is illustrated in Fig 1.3. It consists of a toothed 'crown wheel' mounted on a vertical arbor which is driven by the clock gears and pinions through a 'contrate wheel'. Engaging with the crown wheel are two pallets, A and B, mounted on a pallet arbor which is connected to the pendulum either directly or via a crutch. The included angle between the pallets is typically about 90 degrees but is dependent on various parameters. In action the crown wheel attempts to unwind under the spring/weight action applied to the movement but is restrained from doing so by the pallets A and B. The driving force applied to the pallets/pendulum is transmitted through the vertical faces of the crown wheel. This causes the pendulum to swing back and forth, and in so doing each oscillation releases a tooth on the crown wheel. The movement thus slowly unwinds and the rate at which it does so is regulated by the pendulum.

The verge escapement is generally a relatively poor time keeper compared with other escapements, but when set up correctly will keep reasonably accurate time. The pendulum amplitude is wider than for clocks using the anchor or dead beat escapement.

Anchor escapement

The anchor escapement illustrated in Fig 1.4 was invented about 1670. It was used quite early on longcase clocks, but was not applied to bracket clocks for up to a century later mainly because it is more critical to set up than the verge. The vast majority of pendulum clocks today are fitted with anchor escapements. The mechanism consists of an escape wheel and anchor with pallet ends. The escape wheel typically has 30 teeth with the anchor spanning 7½ teeth. Referring to Fig 1.4 the action is as follows.

Assuming the escape wheel E rotates clockwise driven through the gears and pinions by the spring/weights, this applies the force to the pallets/anchor causing the pendulum to swing from side to side. Unlike the verge where

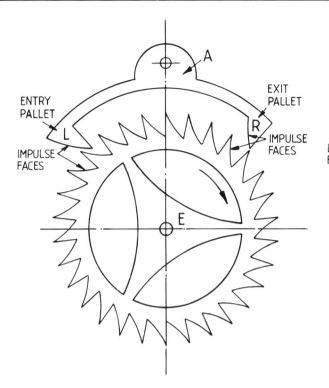

1.4 *Anchor escapement*

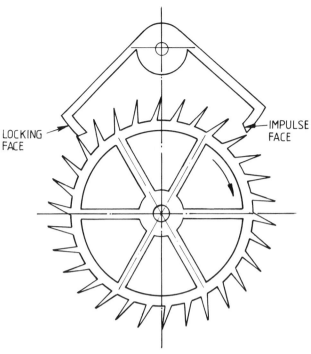

1.5 *Dead beat escapement*

the impulse is applied to the vertical faces of the crown wheel teeth, on the anchor escapement the impulse is through the curved faces of the escape wheel teeth/pallets. The anchor pallets L and R restrain the escape wheel against rapid unwinding, and the pendulum motion back and forth unlocks this a tooth at a time allowing the mechanism to slowly unwind. Each pendulum oscillation applies a slight anti-clockwise motion or 'recoil' to the escape wheel at the end of its travel, before releasing it to turn again in its normal clockwise direction. This is due to the pendulum momentum at the end of its swing, i.e. at highest point, which temporarily overcomes the driving force acting on the pallets.

Dead beat escapement

The dead beat is a precision escapement used on high quality clocks and is illustrated in Fig 1.5. There are several forms, all of which have finely cut wheels and pallet arms. The commonest dead beat is one where the escape wheel teeth are sloped slightly forward in the direction of motion, and the pallet arms have precisely cut ends. The action is similar to the anchor escapement but it does not suffer from 'recoil'. If you study the motion you will see that this

releases and locks the escape wheel teeth in a regular defined manner. It is not generally attributed to any particular horologist though George Graham is said to be the first to have used it successfully in a movement about 1715. If a dial is fitted with a seconds hand this will usually give a clue as to the type of escapement fitted behind. The verge and anchor both recoil and you will see the seconds hand oscillate slightly as it moves round on clocks fitted with these escapements. However, on a clock fitted with a deadbeat escapement this is not observed.

Strikes and chimes

On early movements the hour strike was done using a 'count wheel' while later clocks use 'rack striking'. The count wheel is illustrated in Fig 1.6 and has a series of slots spaced progressively round the rim into which a latch will drop to stop it rotating. This wheel is released on the hour and while the latch is lifted and running along the outer rim, the clock will strike according to the length of time it remains raised. When the latch drops into the next slot the strike terminates. On a rack-striking clock (Fig 1.7) a snail cam on the same arbor as the hour hand is used to preset a toothed rack controlling the

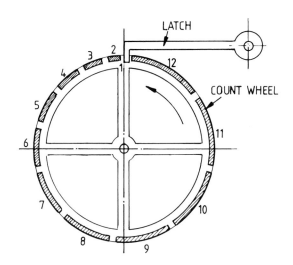

1.6 *Count wheel strike*

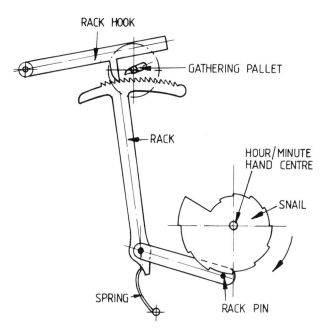

1.7 *Rack strike*

o'clock before moving the hands on or the rack pin will snag on the snail cam. The following is a list of some of the basic strikes and chimes.

Timepiece: A clock which tells the time of day by the dial and hands only and has no strike or chime.

Passing strike: Strikes a single blow on the hour and perhaps also on the half hour.

Hour striking: Strikes the hour on a bell, the number of blows indicating the hour.

Dutch striking: Has two bells, a large low-pitched one to strike the hour, and a smaller high-pitched one to indicate the half hour. At the half hour the succeeding hour is struck on the smaller pitched bell only. Thus half past five would be sounded by six blows on the smaller bell.

Roman striking: Strikes the hour on two bells the higher pitch one striking 'I' and lower pitch one the 'V'. To strike an 'X' two blows are struck on the lower pitched bell. Thus any hour can thus be struck with a maximum of four blows. Devised by Joseph Knibb to reduce strike power demands on long duration clocks, e.g. month going.

Grand-sonnerie: Uses two bells/gongs, one to strike the hour and the other to strike the quarter with one to three blows. A full grand-sonnerie additionally strikes the hour and the quarter hour every fifteen minutes.

Ting-tang: Strikes the quarter on two bells with a sound rather like the name, with additional ting-tangs for each quarter. Thus three quarters of an hour strikes three ting-tangs. Sometimes referred to as bim-bam.

Westminster chime: Chimes the familiar 'Big Ben' strike. Uses four bells.

Whittington chime: Less familiar than 'Big Ben'. Uses eight bells.

St. Michael chime: First quarter is similar to Whittington but thereafter differs.

Movement selection

Although this book is primarily concerned with the construction of clock casework, consideration nevertheless has to be given to the movement being fitted. Briefly, all movements are made to a price and as with most things in life you generally get what you pay for. Thus if you purchase a cheap movement you cannot expect it to last a lifetime because plainly it will

number of hourly strikes. On the hour the strike mechanism is triggered and a gathering pallet progressively collects up the rack a tooth at a time for each strike required.

The count-wheel striking system has the disadvantage that it can get unsynchronized with the hands. To prevent this, if the clock has stopped and the hands need resetting, these clocks should be made to sound the hour before moving on to the next. A clock with a rack-strike mechanism, however, is much less susceptible to getting out of step with the hour hand, though it must be allowed to strike 12

11

not. Also, while strikes and chimes may perhaps be important their incorporation into movements can mean that you can end up paying more for this part of the motion than for the going train alone, maybe at loss of quality as regards the latter.

Spring and weight driven movements are generally available for durations of 30 hours (one day) or eight days (one week), and the market is principally aimed at the latter. With regard to movement design it is not always appreciated that the driving torque applied by the spring or weights often applies a substantial force to the gears and the pinions. This torque transmitted between the gear and pinion teeth is then reacted on the front and back plates at the ends of the arbors (i.e. the bearings) and this can cause distortion of the frame and increased friction in the movement.

A well engineered movement should ideally have thick front and back plates made from half hard brass, which are rigidly connected by substantial pillars to resist twisting. This will help to reduce friction and minimize wear on the arbors, gears and pinions. Many movements today have thin plates and should preferably be avoided, or at least given careful consideration before selection. The gears and pinions should also be made from compatible materials, i.e. half hard brass for the gears and high carbon steel or case hardened steel for the arbors. Arbors made of low carbon steel will quickly wear away at the pivot ends. On some of the higher quality movements available the arbors fit into jewelled bearings and the escapement pallets may also be jewelled. Frictional forces on arbors can be reduced by polishing the arbor ends which will reduce wear and increase life.

To sum up, first check the specification and the materials used to construct the movement. Second, find out what length of guarantee the manufacturer offers on the movement – five, ten or forty years – and make sure you have an arrangement of strikes and chimes suited to the clock case design. Third, remember that a finely built, well engineered movement will on average last rather longer than one made for the cheaper end of the market. You may not get answers to all your questions, but this is sometimes because the supplier often cannot tell you without reference to the manufacturer. If all else fails, then at least you will have tried before making the all-important decision on which movement to fit.

Finally, on the matter of movement lubrication, never apply this to gears and pinions but only to the arbor bearings using a fine grade horological oil.

TABLE
CLOCKS

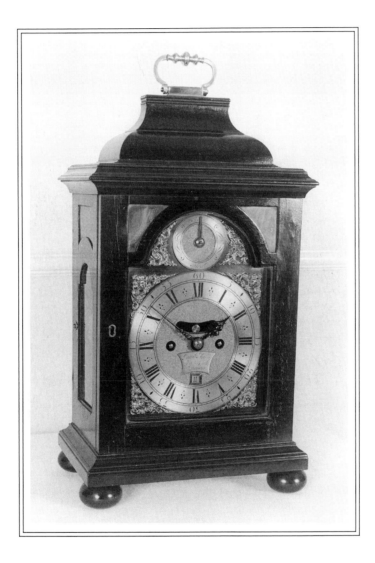

CHAPTER 2

Daniel Quare bracket clock
c.1690

The first few chapters of this book I have devoted to six designs of English bracket clocks presented in roughly chronological order. Besides the constructional aspects I will also discuss at the appropriate point how the particular case design evolved. The very earliest bracket clock cases were rather like houses and had architectural style tops. However, these are quite rare, so I am going to begin in this chapter with a late seventeenth century dome top bracket clock by Daniel Quare which can be seen on display at Lyme Park, Cheshire (N.T.). This impressive country house is approached by a long winding drive from nearby Disley, and it contains the renowned Francis Legh clock collection. Sir Francis Legh, who donated Lyme Park to the nation in 1984, had a lifetime interest in horology, and the resulting collection he made of English bracket and longcase clocks is probably among the best in Britain.

What I particularly like about the bracket clock section is the way the cases and associated movements are displayed separately, which permits you to view them on all sides. Possibly the most important bracket clock is a very early architectural style ebonized clock c.1658 by Ahasuerus Fromanteel. The collection also includes a number of late seventeenth century ebonized bracket clocks by famous makers such as Thomas Tompion, Joseph Knibb, Edward East and Daniel Quare. The movements are of the highest quality with richly engraved backplates, and striking arrangements such as Roman, Dutch and grand-sonnerie. Externally the clocks have equally impressive dials and spandrels, and the dome tops on some are adorned with basket weave decoration and fire-gilt finials. The particular bracket clock design I have selected to feature is No. 8 in the collection

2.1 *Daniel Quare bracket clock*

c.1690, which although it has a complex movement and dial has a simple case to make.

Daniel Quare was born in London in 1647 and became a brother of the Clockmakers Company in 1670. By 1680 he was producing watches as well as clocks, and he continued to make both throughout his career. He had a workshop in Exchange Alley and during part of his life worked in partnership with another clockmaker Stephen Horseman. Quare was a quaker and refused the office of clockmaker to

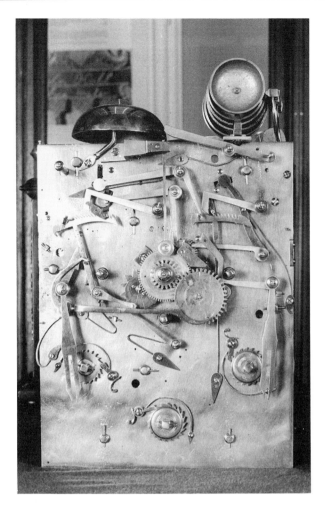

2.2 Movement of Daniel Quare bracket clock

2.3 Side view of Daniel Quare movement

George I because he objected to the oath of allegiance to the King. Court protocol was eventually overcome by allowing Daniel Quare free admittance to the King via the back stairs of the Palace.

Clock and movement

The clock has a three train, spring wound fusee movement, with a verge escapement and a lenticular bob pendulum with rise and fall suspension/regulation. The back plate is profusely engraved and signed in an oval reserve 'Daniel Quare, London'. The grand-sonnerie quarter strike is on six bells. The dial plate has a matted centre with a false pendulum opening, ringed winding holes and a square calender aperture. The four small dials at the corners make this an extremely versatile clock. In the top left corner is the 'pen/reg' dial operating a mechanical device which raises and lowers the

pendulum to swing faster or slower. To the top right is a pendulum locking device to stop the movement during transit, operated by the 'pen fast/pen loose' dial. The dial in the bottom left is the 'silent/strike', allowing you to stop the clock chiming altogether, and to its right is the 'repeat/ not repeat' dial to silence the grand-sonnerie chime, leaving it to strike only the hours.

Case design

The clock case is of square dial form with a dial plate nominally 200mm (8in) square, and doors front and rear to give access for winding and setting the pendulum in motion. Around the base is a moulded surround and above the dial is a pierced fretwork panel which is repeated on the sides (Fig 2.4). The top of the clock is of dome form above a moulded coving. The case is fitted with a handle and pineapple finials in the corners, and stands on square form pad feet.

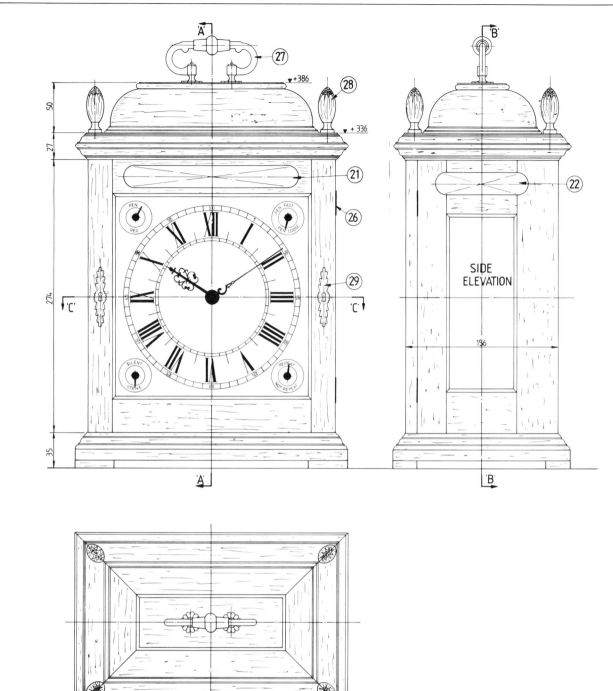

2.4 (Below) *Pierced fretwork detail*

2.5 (Above) *General arrangement of Daniel Quare bracket clock*

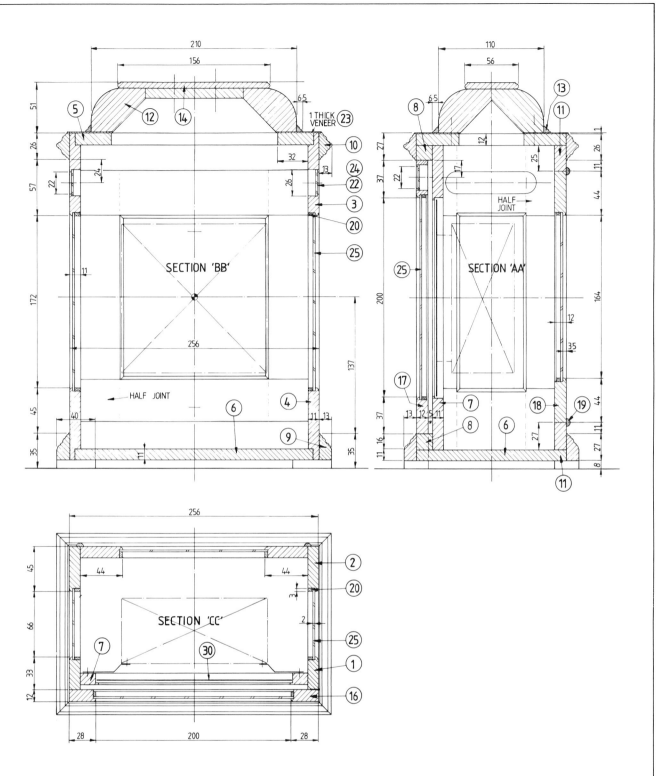

Construction

The general arrangement is given in Fig 2.5 with sectional details in Fig 2.6. In addition a rear view is given in Fig 2.7. Moulding profile details are shown in Fig 2.8 which also includes a drawing of the pierced fretwork pattern shown on a 5mm squared background.

The original case material I believe is a

2.6 *Sectional arrangement of Daniel Quare bracket clock*

fruitwood, possibly pear. A clue to this was the light case weight and the visible tinges of pink showing here and there through the internal matt black finish. The archives describe the case exterior as ebony veneered which was difficult to verify but is assumed to be correct.

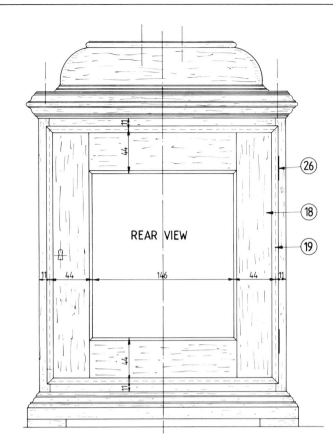

2.7 Details of rear door

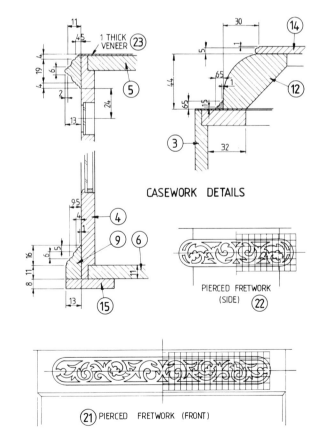

2.8 Moulding and pierced fretwork details

Framework

Begin construction by making the case framework which consists of two half jointed sidelight frames connected together by a top (5) and bottom (6). Square this arrangement up internally by adding the dial mask frame (7) which is also half jointed. Next rebate the mask frame behind to fit the dial plate, or alternatively apply a 2mm thick veneer to the front of this which will achieve the same objective. You should also add the spacer strips (8) and back rails (11) at this stage. Then move on to construct the front and rear doors. These are half jointed frames which you make in a similar way to the sidelights. The front door fits across the full width of the case, while you fit the rear one between the sidelights. Apply half round beading (19) round the edge of the rear door frame to cover the jamb. Next prepare the top of the case ready for the cushion top by first making and gluing on the cove edge moulding (10), and then apply an ebony veneer overlay across the top of this. Also make the base moulding (9) and fit this round the bottom of the case. The form of the coving is a bead with an ogee either side, and that for item (9) is a double ogee over an ovolo. The latter most likely consists of a thin shaped strip of ebony glued onto a pear wood base and ideally this is the way you should make it.

Mouldings and fretwork

Make up the dome top in sections to the details shown. The principal items for this are the cushion top piece (12), cover panel (14) and the corner beading (13). Prepare the cushion top (12) in one long strip and ebony veneer this externally before dividing it up and fitting it. The original cover panel (14) most probably has an applied beaded edging of solid ebony, and I have assumed there is an ebony veneer across the top. The form of the ebony corner beading (13) round the base of the cushion top is an ogee over an ovolo.

Next make the pierced fretwork for the front and sides from 2mm thick ebony strips. Cut this out using a fret saw fitted with a fine toothed blade (40 tpi). You need to use a fine blade to cut a clean edge which also minimizes clean up work afterwards. You could cut both side fretwork panels together by gluing the second strip onto the first using scotch glue with a paper sandwich in between, though I prefer to make them individually. Afterwards gently soak in water to break the joint and clean off the paper. Polish the fretwork pieces afterwards on a flat surface before fixing them in the appropriate panel. Incidentally the fretwork design appears to be a fairly common pattern used about this period, and recently I came across an almost identical shape on a bracket clock by John Bushman of London dated 1695.

Dial and movement

It is obviously not going to be possible to incorporate a dial and movement of the original quality and modern day movements will have to be substituted. Fit an eight day spring wound pendulum regulated movement and 200mm square dial plate of the best quality. Dial plates, chapter rings and movements do vary among manufacturers, and you should obtain these items at the start of the project so that any minor alterations to the case framework can be accommodated. The thickness of the front spacer strip (8) is dependent upon the movement and the space needed for the hands. In Chapter 3 I have given some notes on the general principles of fixing bracket clock dial plates and movements. Finally, this particular bracket clock is one of the larger ones, but they were also made to suit the other dial sizes such as 150mm (6in) and 115mm (4½in) square. If you would like to make a smaller variation then you should reduce the case size proportionately.

PARTS LIST

Item	No	Material	Dimensions (mm)
### *Casework*			
1 Sidelight stile (1)	2	Pear	33×11×327 long
2 Sidelight stile (2)	2	Pear	45×11×327 long
3 Sidelight rail (1)	2	Pear	83×11×144 long
4 Sidelight rail (2)	2	Pear	72×11×144 long
5 Case top	1	Pear	45×11×810 long total. Half jointed framework
6 Case bottom	1	Pear	156×12×245 long
7 Dial plate frame	1	Pear	Sides 20×11×304 long Top/bottom 55×11×234 long
8 Spacer strip	2	Pear	17×16×234 long
9 Base edging	1	Pear	27×13×950 long total
10 Cove edging	1	Pear	26×13×950 long total
11 Back rail	2	Pear	27×13×256 long
12 Cushion top moulding	1	Pear	75×38×700 long total
13 Corner beading	1	Pear	7sq×750 long total
14 Cover panel	1	Pear	120×7×220 long
15 Foot pad	4	Pear	25×8×180 long for all four pads
16 Front door stile	2	Pear	28×12×274 long
17 Front door rail	2	Pear	37×12×256 long
18 Rear door frame	1	Pear	44×12×1000 long total
19 Door bead surround	1	Pear	7×4×1050 long total
20 Beading	1	Pear	5×3×2600 long total
21 Pierced fret panel (1)	1	Ebony	26×2×200 long
22 Pierced fret panel (2)	2	Ebony	26×2×110 long
23 Veneer	–	Ebony	Quantity to suit case exterior
24 Fret back cloth	–	Red silk	Purchase to suit
### *Glass*			
25 Door & sidelight glass	–	Picture glass	Quantity to suit front/rear doors and sidelights

Metalwork

No	Item	Qty	Material	Notes
26	Hinge	4	Brass	20×10 wide nominal size
27	Carrying handle	1	Brass	95×38 nominal size
28	Pineapple finial	4	Brass	Purchase to suit
29	Escutcheon plate	2	Brass	Purchase to suit
30	Dial plate	1	–	200sq nominal size
31	Hands	1 pair	Blued steel	Purchase to suit
32	Movement	1	–	Eight day spring wound c/w pendulum

CHAPTER 3

Arch dial bracket clock

(c.1720)

At beginning of the eighteenth century changes occurred in bracket clock case design. The dial remained square for about ten years up to about 1710, but then another style developed where the top had a distinctive bell shape. It was very simple really, in that a concave wood section was added above the earlier dome form and thus its shape changed into an 'inverted bell top'. At the same time a complementary true 'bell top' style was also developed by reversing the curve, making the original dome section concave and the new top section convex. Fig 3.1 illustrates the way clock case style changed from the early architectural top of around 1670 as in (A), to the dome top about 1675 in (B), then to the 'inverted bell top' as in (C). In the fully

developed bell top form the square dial plate also changed to an 'arch dial' where the arch mirrored to a degree the bell shape top and made an aesthetically pleasing arrangement (D). Pierced fretting was often fitted either side of the dial arch to fill the corner space. Arch dial bell top clocks are thus generally taller than their square dial counterparts.

Fig 3.2 shows how the introduction of the bell top also changed the appearance of case sides. The earliest case sides c.1670 had a plain glass aperture as in (A). By 1690 pierced fretwork above the dial had been introduced and this was reflected in the sidelight as in (B). Sometimes the sidelight was split into two glazed frames with the smaller one at the top as (C). When arch dial

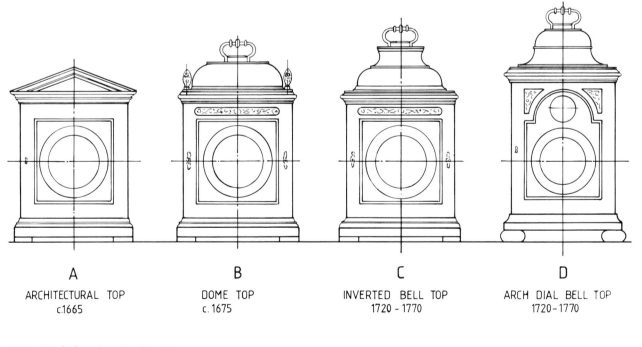

A	B	C	D
ARCHITECTURAL TOP	DOME TOP	INVERTED BELL TOP	ARCH DIAL BELL TOP
c.1665	c.1675	1720 - 1770	1720-1770

3.1 *Early bracket clock styles*

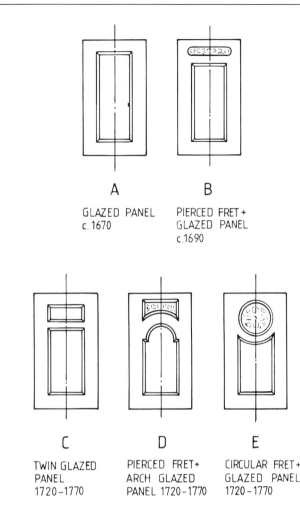

A

GLAZED PANEL
c. 1670

B

PIERCED FRET +
GLAZED PANEL
c.1690

C

TWIN GLAZED
PANEL
1720 – 1770

D

PIERCED FRET +
ARCH GLAZED
PANEL 1720 – 1770

E

CIRCULAR FRET +
GLAZED PANEL
1720 – 1770

3.2 *Bracket clock sidelights*

clocks were introduced with their taller cases it was a natural development then to form a glazed arch in the side as in (D), as this too mirrored the bell top shape when the clock was viewed from the side. An alternative to this was a circular pierced fret above a glazed aperture with a concave top, as in E.

Bell top clocks were popular for some sixty years or so with an ebonized finish over an oak or pear wood case. With oak, which does not take an ebonized finish easily, it was generally better to apply ebony veneer on top. Pear wood on the other hand will produce an excellent ebonized surface, and an external ebonized veneer over the case was not necessary. Bracket clocks were also made with walnut veneered cases in the early part of the eighteenth century, and between 1725–1750 japanned casework is found. By 1770 mahogany casework had began to predominate, but ebonized cases still persisted until quite late in the century.

Case design

The design here is measured from a bell top arch dial clock c.1720 as shown in Figs 3.3 and 3.4, and is suited to a 150mm nominal diameter dial. The case has many of the features mentioned above, an inverted bell top, arched window sidelights and front and rear doors. The clock stands on bun feet which were a common feature on furniture of the walnut period 1680–1720, and the casework is oak with external ebony veneering. Either side of the arch and also in the sidelight top openings are pinkish-brown pear wood panels. It is thought that these panels might have originally been pierced fretwork openings which maybe became broken. All the glazed apertures on the front, rear and sides are framed with pear wood beading left its natural colour.

3.3 *Arch dial bracket clock*

3.4 Sidelight of arch dial bracket clock

3.5 Engraved backplate of Jacob Malsey movement

Dial and movement

The original movement is spring wound, fitted with a verge escapement, calendar work and a repeat strike facility. The brass dial plate has an applied chapter ring, a false pendulum opening in the middle and is signed 'Jacob Malsey, Leicester Fields, London'. The arch sections were often purely decorative but this clock features a silent/strike setting with spandrels to either side. The corner spandrels were difficult to decipher but appear to be a version of the female head typically 1715–1745.

Case construction

The general arrangement drawings are given in Fig 3.6, and sectional details in Fig 3.7. As mentioned earlier the original case is oak, but if you want to avoid the complication of ebony veneering over this then change this to pear. Begin construction by first preparing the sidelights (1) which are cut from solid panels, and fit these to the top and bottom items (2), (3), (4). Next stiffen up this arrangement with a half jointed dial plate mask frame made to details as shown in Fig. 3.8. The top items (2) and (3) are shown as a half jointed assembly but this is optional, and you could make the construction simpler by using a one piece wood panel if required. Before you glue the mask frame and the case surround together, add a thick ebony veneer to the front of the mask to form a rebate for the dial plate to fit behind. It is much easier to do this while the mask is a free item. The original dial plate is approximately 172mm square and 233mm over the arch. You may need to adjust the case dimensions if the dial plate fitted differs from this.

The front and rear doors are half jointed frames to details as in Fig 3.8. It was uncertain what the timber was for the bun feet. They are unlikely to be real ebony and it is suggested that they are turned from pear with an ebonized finish. Use dowels to fit them to the case.

Mouldings

Make up the bell top from moulding sections as indicated. The bell top strip moulding (16) has a bead edge top and bottom with an ogee in between. The bead strip (17) is an ogee

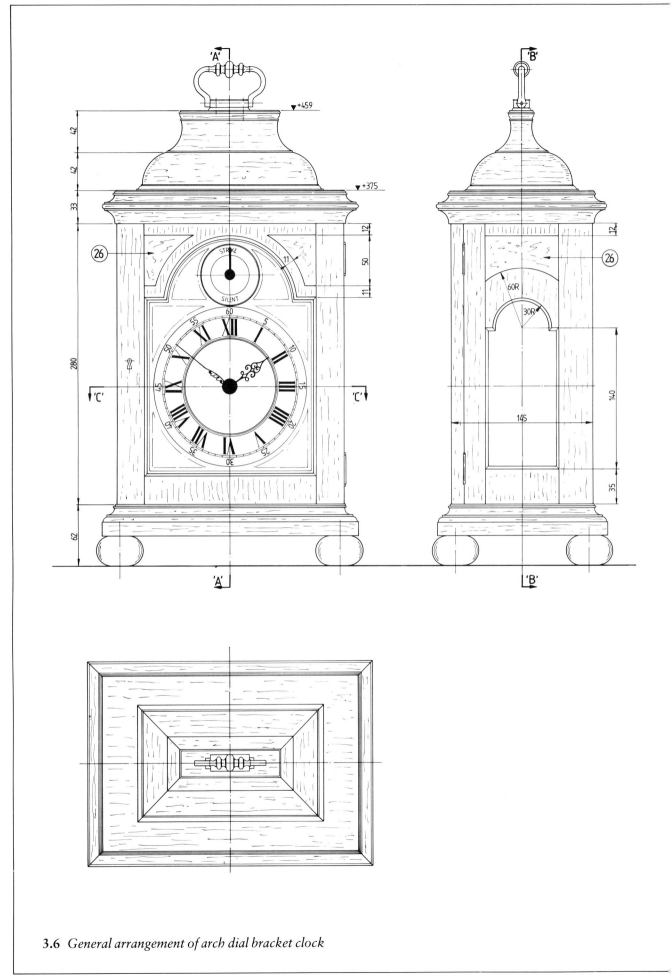

3.6 *General arrangement of arch dial bracket clock*

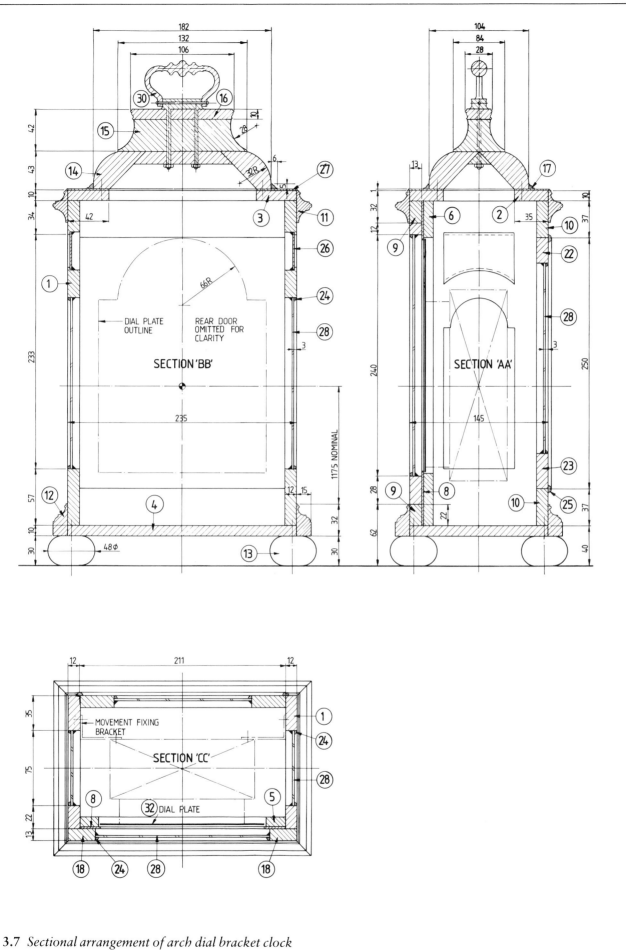

3.7 *Sectional arrangement of arch dial bracket clock*

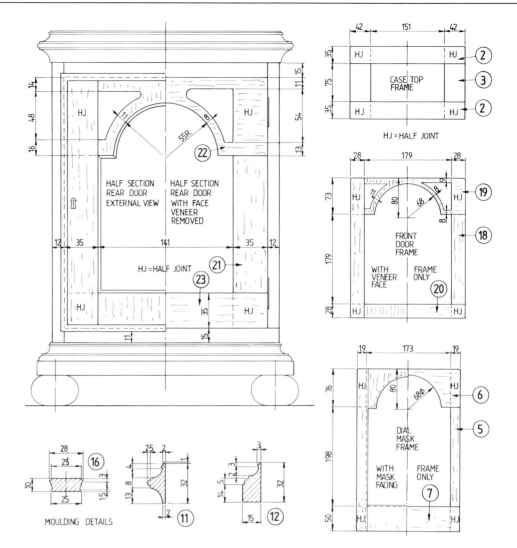

3.8 Miscellaneous details of arch dial bracket clock

moulding. On the case, the cove moulding (11) is a bead with a coving either side, and the base moulding (12) is a bead/coving over an ovolo.

Glazed panels

A general point to note is the fixing of the glazed panels. On early clocks glass was held in by a coloured putty to suit the wood, and there is no reason why you should not do the same again. Today ready made coloured putties are available. Wood beading to hold glass into place is generally of a later date.

Fixing bracket clock movements

On most period bracket clocks the mechanical part comprising the dial plate and the movement is considered as a composite unit separate from

the case. The method of assembly is very similar to that used on longcase clocks, except that where bracket clocks are concerned the dial/movement is offered into the case from the back and fixed with brackets in various ways as illustrated in Fig 3.9.

Considering first the assembly of the movement and dial plate, these two are normally 'posted' together by four short pillars which are riveted into the back of the dial plate. These pillars have shouldered ends which pass through matching holes in the corners of the movement front plate. A small pin is then fixed through the transverse hole in each pillar end behind the front plate, thus locking the two together. The space between the dial plate and the movement front plate varies typically being 15 to 30mm but depends on the arrangement. The hands are then added, the hour hand fitting on the 'cannon pin', and the minute hand in front on the centre pin fixed by another small cross pin. The dial/

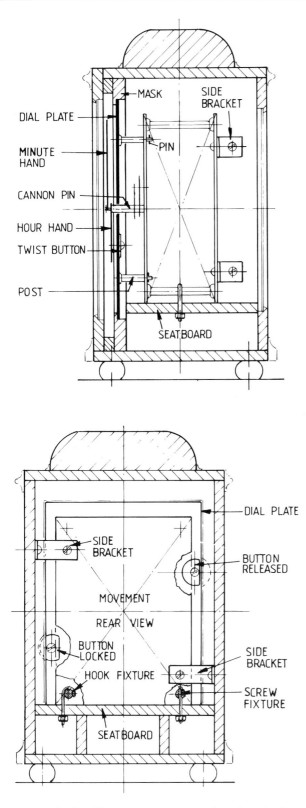

3.9 *Methods of fixing movements to bracket clock cases*

secured to its case in one of two ways. The first is to place the movement on a wooden platform known as 'seatboard'. This is then secured either by a screw rod arrangement passing through the bottom pillars or a 'J' hook screw fixture clamping over these. The second method, where there is no seatboard as in the arch dial clock here, is to fix angle brackets to the movement which are then screwed internally to the casework. There is a further subsidiary method which is to hold the movement via its dial plate into the mask framework using small metal discs or buttons which fit into a groove or recess in the mask frame. These 'buttons' which are screw fixed into the back of the dial plate edge have a flat on one side. When the dial plate is correctly positioned the buttons are twisted to lock them into the mask frame grooves. This method of fixing is less common than the others, and often requires the addition of internal supporting brackets as mentioned above to help carry the weight of the movement.

While the above summarizes the conventional method of fixing period bracket clock movements, I should mention that modern movements produced today are not often provided with posts to secure the dial plate onto it, and the two components are therefore fixed separately to the case. In this arrangement the movement is still fixed using the methods outlined above, but the dial plate is secured separately onto the mask. The usual way of fixing the dial plate is by means of small pins or screws through holes on the perimeter edges onto the front of a solid mask board. Alternatively you can fix the dial plate from behind into the mask frame rebate and hold it in place with wood beading. The hands are then added on to the motionwork as described above.

movement as a unit is then offered to the case from the back, the dial plate fitting in the recess behind the mask frame.

A bracket clock movement is normally

PARTS LIST

Item	No	Material	Dimensions (mm)
Casework			
1 Sidelight	2	Oak	133×10×324 long
2 Case top strip (1)	2	Oak	35×10×235 long
3 Case top strip (2)	2	Oak	42×10×145 long

No.	Description	Qty	Material	Dimensions / Notes
4	Case bottom	1	Oak	145×10×235 long
5	Dial mask side strip	2	Oak	19×10×324 long
6	Dial mask top strip	1	Oak	76×10×211 long
7	Dial mask bottom strip	1	Oak	50×10×211 long
8	Mask face strip	1	Pear	160×2×350 long. Cut out & fit to suit
9	Front door sill strip	2	Oak	22×12×211 long
10	Rear door sill strip	2	Oak	37×12×211 long
11	Cove moulding	1	Pear	32×15×950 long total
12	Base moulding	1	Pear	32×15×950 long total
13	Bun foot	4	Pear	50sq×200 long for all four pads. Spigot fit
14	Bell top moulding (1)	1	Pear	70×28×600 long total
15	Bell top moulding (2)	1	Pear	60×32×115 long
16	Bell top strip	1	Pear	30×10×115 long
17	Roof ogee bead	1	Pear	6×5×650 long
18	Front door stile	2	Oak	28×13×280 long
19	Front door top rail	1	Oak	73×13×235 long
20	Front door bottom rail	1	Oak	28×13×235 long
21	Rear door stile	2	Oak	35×12×250 long
22	Rear door top rail	1	Oak	73×12×211 long
23	Rear door bottom rail	1	Oak	35×12×211 long
24	Beading	1	Pear	3sq×2500 long total. Do not ebonize
25	Door lipping	1	Pear	8×4×1000 long total
26	Panel insets	–	Pear	Quantity to suit front, back & side of case. Do not ebonize
27	Veneer	–	Pear	Veneer all over case & ebonize finish

Glass

No.	Description	Qty	Material	Dimensions / Notes
28	Door & sidelight glass	–	Picture glass	Cut to suit front/rear doors and sidelights

Metalwork

No.	Description	Qty	Material	Dimensions / Notes
29	Hinge	4	Brass	25×10 wide nominal size
30	Carrying handle	1	Brass	76×38 nominal size
31	Escutcheon	2	Brass	Purchase to suit
32	Dial plate	1	Brass	173sq nominal size c/w arch top
33	Chapter ring	1	Silvered brass	160 nominal O.D.
34	Corner spandrel	4	Brass	Purchase to suit
35	Arch spandrel	1 pair	Brass	Purchase to suit
36	Hands	1 pair	Blued steel	Purchase to suit
37	Movement	1	–	Eight day spring wound c/w pendulum

CHAPTER 4

Regency bracket clock (c. 1810)

Towards the end of the eighteenth century the popularity of square dials waned and round white dial clocks became fashionable. The predominant case material by then was mahogany introduced around 1750. Better quality cases in the Sheraton period were inlaid with exotic woods, and later Regency brass inlay became popular. Case styles changed accordingly to suit the round dial, the most common of which is the so-called 'broken arch' form. These cases introduced around 1780 had a round top the curve of which is broken at the sides by two flat shoulders, hence the name. Fig 4.1 gives the principal variations of the 1780–1820 period. Fig 4.1(A) shows the 'broken arch' clock with its round top, shoulders and fretwork below the dial, (B) the true 'round top' with an unbroken curve to the sides, (C) the 'lancet' style clock case with a curved pointed top, and (D) the 'balloon' clock.

These clocks also had distinctive side panels as shown in Fig 4.2. Common patterns were rectangular or arched openings either glazed, or with pierced wooden fretwork, or with gothic style brass fretting. The fretwork was backed by silk material which was usually red, yellow, blue or purple.

Case design

Broken arch bracket clock dials range typically from 120 to 200mm in diameter. The design in this chapter is for a larger style bracket clock as shown in Figs 4.3 and 4.4. The case is principally oak with mahogany veneer externally and moulded edging around the top, sides and base. The clock is nominally 381mm (15in) high and features brass fretwork panels on the front and sides. The fretwork panels have

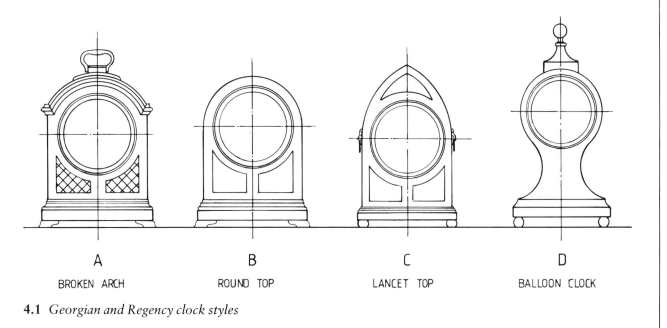

A	B	C	D
BROKEN ARCH	ROUND TOP	LANCET TOP	BALLOON CLOCK

4.1 *Georgian and Regency clock styles*

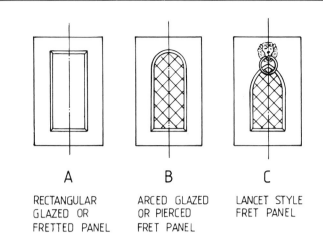

A
RECTANGULAR
GLAZED OR
FRETTED PANEL

B
ARCED GLAZED
OR PIERCED
FRET PANEL

C
LANCET STYLE
FRET PANEL

4.2 Georgian and Regency clock sidelights

4.4 Detail of fish scale fretwork

a fish scale pattern with a red silk backing. Access to the dial for winding is via a hinged front door having a fixed glazed bezel. The rear access door has a plain glazed panel. The case top is 'coopered' which is an applied strip form of construction. The clock stands on ogee pattern brass feet.

4.3 Broken arch bracket clock

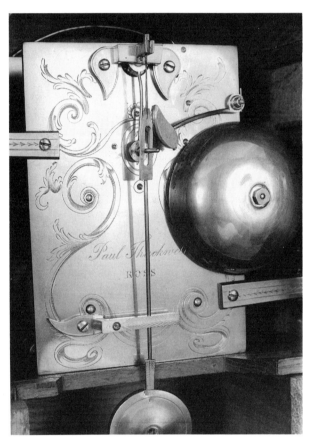

4.5 Engraved backplate of Paul Thackwell movement

Dial and movement

The four pillar movement has an anchor escapement with pendulum regulation, and has rack-striking with a repeat facility. The eight day spring wound movement has fusee compensation. The convex painted white dial plate is signed 'Paul Thackwell, Ross-on-Whye'. The engraved backplate of the movement is shown in Fig 4.5.

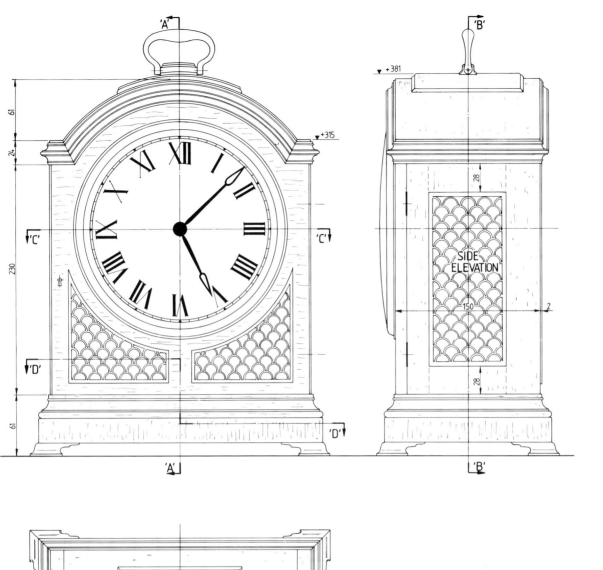

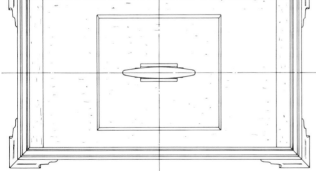

4.6 *General arrangement of Regency bracket clock*

Construction

The general arrangement drawings are given in Fig 4.6 with principal sections in Fig 4.7. A half section view of the front and rear door framing is shown in Fig 4.8. Miscellaneous details of the sidelight framing, mouldings and ogee feet are

shown in Fig 4.9. The case is designed to suit a dial plate size 200mm O.D. and the minute ring O.D. is 186mm. If the dial plate size fitted differs from this you may need to modify the casework dimensions to maintain the correct proportions.

Commence construction by making the 10mm thick sidelight frames, items (1), (2), (3) and (4)

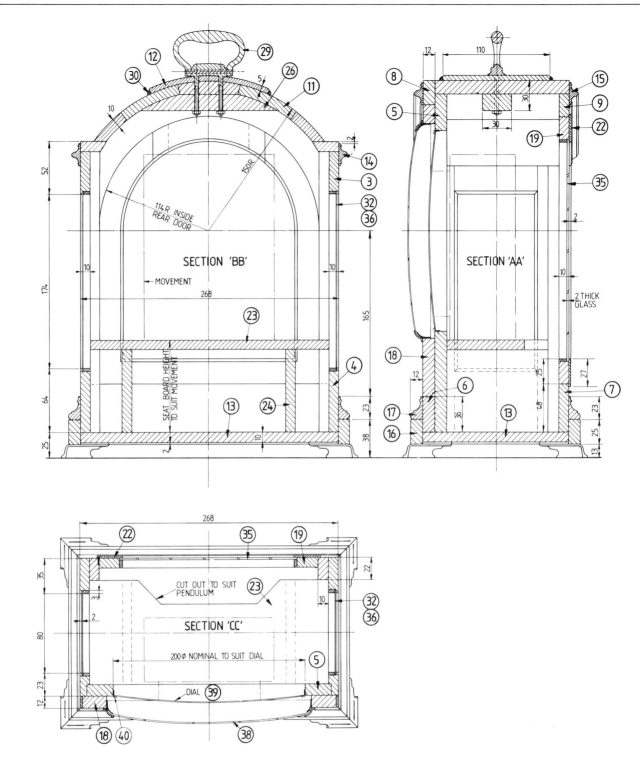

4.7 *Sectional arrangement of Regency bracket clock*

using half joint connection at the corners. You should rebate these frame strips internally to fit the brass fretting prior to assembly. There are two ways you can do this, either by cutting the rebate directly into the wood strip as shown on the drawing, or by gluing a strip of 2mm thick mahogany veneer on the outside of the sidelight.

The latter was how the original clock was made, and indeed many period bracket clock frames are rebated this way. You can make the sidelights like this by cutting thin magohany strips to suit and gluing these on. An easier solution is to use constructional veneer which is thicker than normal veneer and about the right

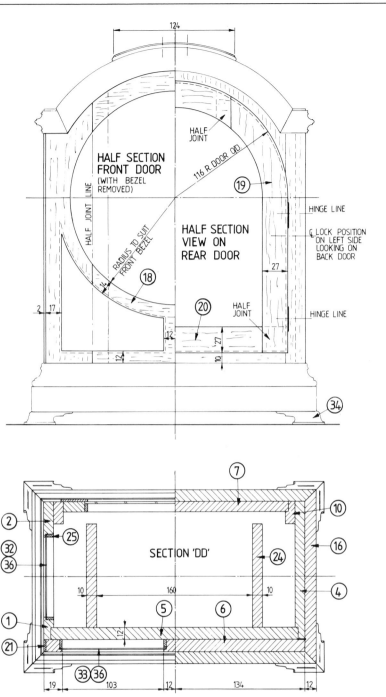

4.8 *Front and rear door details and cross section 'DD'*

thickness required. By careful planning you can make the sidelight framework in longer strips and then divide up to suit. Before making up these panels check the availability of the fish scale pattern brass fretwork which may affect the size of the openings in these. See the notes on fretting alternatives below.

With the sidelights complete move on to prepare other items including the base (13), dial mask panel (5), and case rear framework. Connect these with half joints and rebate them

as shown on the drawings. At this stage you should also prepare the coopered roof strips (11). When work is complete on these items you can then attempt a preliminary assembly, checking for fitness and squareness etc. You will find jigs in the form of spacing blocks between the front and back framework are useful to assist in setting these together correctly. Make sure the centre cut out in the dial mask panel (5) is an accurate fit for the dial plate bezel ring (40). This will save later re-work when access is more

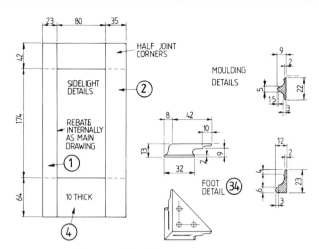

4.9 Miscellaneous details

difficult on the glued assembly. When the fit is satisfactory dismantle for gluing, reclamp and leave aside to set. After the casework has set assemble the coopered roof strips (11), and after checking they will fit neatly together glue these in place.

Miscellaneous fittings

Once you have cleaned up the case you can then add other items stage by stage. This includes the front door sill (6), arch rail (8), bottom rail/edge moulding (16), (17), and the coving strips (14, 15). The cove moulding form is a bead with a coving/small bead either side, and the base moulding is a coving/small bead over an ovolo. There are two ways to make the arch moulding, either by woodturning from a thin disc, or alternatively by machine routing with the router set up on a suitable radius arm. The front and rear doors are mahogany frames fretsawn and half jointed to details as in Fig 4.8. Take especial care when you cut out the front door frame as this is somewhat fragile, but it will stiffen up when you fit the frets.

Fretwork panels

Brass fretwork in the fish scale pattern is available commercially (see List of suppliers), but you may have to get them cut to order specifying the size required. Alternatively if you feel sufficiently skilled you could cut the brass frets. To do this first prepare the brass plates by applying engineers' marking ink and accurately mark out the pattern with scribers and

compasses. Next drill a hole in each fish scale opening large enough to get a saw blade through, and then carefully enlarge each hole to the finished size. Use a fine toothed piercing saw to do this to give a good finish with the minimum of re-work.

If either of these approaches still gives you problems there are other solutions to try. You could instead make a pierced wood fret to fit each side panel, or simply glaze these apertures. For the front door you might use pierced wooden frets again, or perhaps make the door with a solid bottom and frame the corner area with brass inlay strip. You could also use a sand shaded fan marquetry motif in the corners. These were all options used by clock case makers during the 1780–1820 period, and so are acceptable alternatives.

Finally, still on the subject of fretwork, it is worth mentioning that besides being decorative it does have a function too, in that the holes through it allow the strike/chime to be heard, whilst the silk backing behind stops the dust from entering the case.

Movement

You should fit an eight day spring wound movement with pendulum regulation. The drawing shows a seatboard fixing but mounting brackets could be used depending on the movement fitted. The dial plate which is posted off the movement should fit neatly behind the bezel ring (40). Alternatively the dial plate can be fixed separately into the bezel (40).

PARTS LIST

Item	No	Material	Dimensions (mm)
Casework			
1 Sidelight stile (1)	2	Oak	23×10×290 long
2 Sidelight stile (2)	2	Oak	35×10×290 long
3 Sidelight rail (1)	2	Oak	42×10×138 long
4 Sidelight rail (2)	2	Oak	64×10×138 long
5 Dial mask panel	1	Oak	254×12×291 long

No.	Part	Qty	Material	Size/Description
6	Door sill (1)	1	Oak	36×12×254 long
7	Door sill (2)	1	Oak	48×10×234 long
8	Door arch rail (1)	1	Oak	75×12×254 long
9	Door arch rail (2)	1	Oak	248×10×150 long
10	Door side strip	2	Oak	22×10×266 long
11	Roof strip	1	Oak	65×13×850 long total
12	Crown panel	1	Mahogany	110×20×130 long
13	Base	1	Oak	150×10×268 long
14	Cove side moulding (1)	1	Mahogany	23×9×550 long total
15	Cove arch moulding (2)	2	Mahogany	100×9×260 long
16	Bottom rail	1	Mahogany	25×12×950 long total
17	Bottom edge moulding (3)	1	Mahogany	23×12×950 long total
18	Front door panel	1	Mahogany	110×12×900 long total
19	Rear door panel	1	Mahogany	75×10×670 long
20	Rear door bottom rail	1	Mahogany	25×10×228 long
21	Door edging	1	Mahogany	12×2×500 long total
22	Door facing	1	Mahogany	65×2×850 long total
23	Seat board	1	Oak	104×10×248 long
24	Seat board support	2	Oak	104×10×85 long
25	Beading	1	Oak	7×3×2000 long total
26	Handle support strip	1	Oak	30×16×150 long
27	Veneer	–	Mahogany	Quantity to suit Veneer all over case

Metalwork

No.	Part	Qty	Material	Size/Description
28	Door hinge	4	Brass	10 wide×25 long
29	Carrying handle	1	Brass	75×40 nominal size. Purchase to suit
30	Brass roof beading	1	Brass	3 mm convex pattern×520 long
31	Lock	2	Brass	Purchase to suit
32	Sidelight fret	2	Brass	180×75 nominal size. Fish scale pattern. Purchase to suit
33	Front door fret	2	Brass	Size as per drawing. Fish scale pattern. Purchase to suit
34	Foot	4	Brass	Purchase to suit

Glass & cloth

No.	Part	Qty	Material	Size/Description
35	Rear door glass	1	Picture glass	Cut to suit
36	Fret back cloth	–	Red silk	300sq. Purchase to suit

Movement

No.	Part	Qty	Material	Size/Description
37	Clock movement	1	–	Eight day spring wound striking bracket clock movement
38	Door bezel	1	Brass	Hingeless bezel & glass for front door, 200 nominal size. Purchase to suit
39	Dial plate	1	Metal plate	White dial 200 nominal dia
40	Dial plate bezel	1	Brass	To suit dial plate

CHAPTER 5

Lancet bracket clock

(c. 1800)

Bracket clocks which have arched pointed tops as in Fig 5.1 are known as 'lancet clocks', and the title is derived from their similarity to the shape of a lancet sword which has a curved pointed double edge blade. Aesthetically these cases are not really suited to having a top carrying handle as do dome or bell top bracket clocks, and instead they usually have two handles, one on either side of the case, often of the lions head drop ring pattern. The dial size range is similar to broken arch bracket clocks. This Regency period case is quite a nice small one, so is ideally suited to a mantlepiece.

Case features

The case is 294mm (11⅝in) high and is designed to suit a dial size 114mm (4½in) nominal diameter. The mahogany case has a lancet style top and a stepped base surround, and stands on brass ball feet. There is a glazed access door to the rear and a front opening bezel for winding. The case is veneered externally with mahogany, with that on the front book matched about the vertical centre line.

The front is inlaid with Regency style raised brass inlay panels above and below the dial and contoured to the bezel profile and case outline. The panel below the dial has an inset diamond pattern brass inlay in the centre. The case is framed by brass columns at the corners, above which are small beaded brass corner strips pin fixed to the arches. Around the stepped base is further decoration in the form of a thin brass strip. The fretted openings in each side and the brass frets themselves are of lancet style matching the case. Above each fret is a lion's head handle.

5.1 *Lancet bracket clock*

Dial and movement

The eight day movement has an anchor escapement with pendulum regulation, and is hour striking with a repeat pull cord. It has a white dial plate with moon style hands and is signed 'M.Storr, London'. The five minute intervals on the minute ring are in a diamond pattern matching the case inlay below the dial.

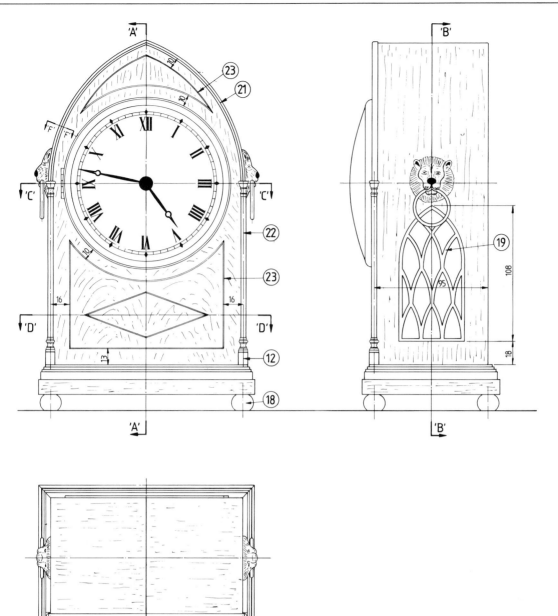

5.2 *General arrangement of lancet bracket clock*

Construction

The general arrangement drawings are given in Fig 5.2 and sectional details in Fig 5.3. A view of the rear door is given in Fig 5.4. The dial plate is 127mm (5in) O.D. and the minute ring is 114mm O.D. If the dial plate size you fit differs from this, the crown radius, case width and possibly the height may be varied to suit. If you choose to make an altogether larger clock to fit say a 150 or 200mm dial you should also consider proportionally increasing the case depth (e.g. 130–150mm). It is perfectly

acceptable to use oak as an alternative case material externally veneered in mahogany, though I suggest that you retain a mahogany frame for the rear door. Ebonized cases were still being made late into the eighteenth century, so another alternative is a pear wood case, either ebonized or with ebony veneer externally, and a matt black finish internally.

The construction is in many ways similar to the broken arch clock detailed in Chapter 4. Commence this by making the side panels (1), bottom (3) and dial board (4). The sides have lancet arch cut outs in the centre rebated to fit

37

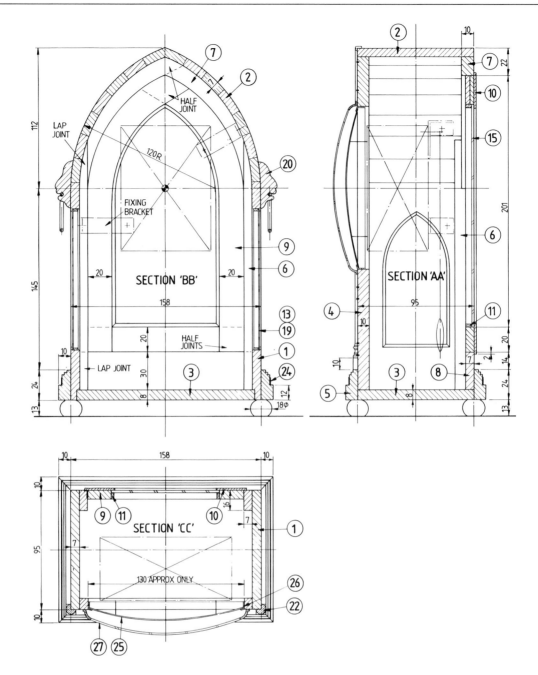

5.3 *Sectional arrangement of lancet bracket clock*

the brass fretting. Check the availability of the brass frets before cutting this opening, and consult the List of suppliers at the back for a suitable source. See also Chapter 4 for suggestions on other alternatives such as pierced wood frets or a glazed aperture. Make sure the opening for the fixed dial plate bezel (26) fits accurately to minimize later re-work when access on the glued assembly is more difficult.

Next prepare the case rear framework comprising the side strips (6), arch strips (7) and sill rail (8). Use a lap joint between the case sides and the arch strips/sill rails/and half joint the

arch strips at the apex. Take care when cutting out and fitting these components together as I found the framework a little fragile. Before gluing check that the frame profile is identical to the dial board (4). In making and gluing together small items like these I find it useful to have a selection of 25 or 50mm screw clamps to hand which are less cumbersome to fix than larger ones. Another method to glue the rear frame is to lay it on a board weighted down over the glued joints. Place a piece of paper between the frame and the board so that if the glue oozes out the joints the frame cannot stick to the board!

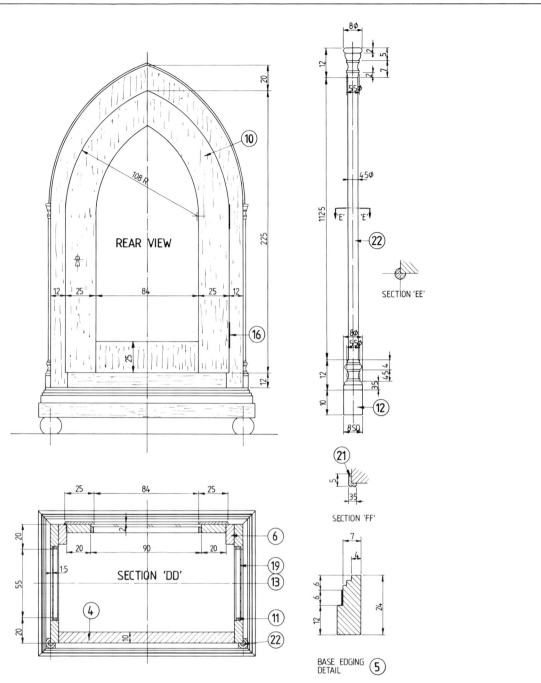

5.4 *Miscellaneous details*

Assembly

With the principal components completed you can proceed to assemble and glue the case together. When set and cleaned up then add the roof strips (2) and afterwards smooth these down to the arch profile. At this point veneer the case externally. Lay the side veneer vertically to minimize the risk of cracks appearing later should the coopering strips shrink a little due to

humidity changes. You will find the veneer will bend quite easily to the arch profile but will need clamping down whilst the glue sets.

Inlay work

Complete the inlay work on the dial board (4) before adding further fittings while access is easy. The normal method of cutting grooves for straight edge inlay work is by means of a home made jig in the form of a double knife made from pair of sharpened hacksaw blades fitted face together in a wooden handle. The blades are bevel ground internally to form the two cutting edges. Use a clamped straight edge as a guide, and for the radiused grooves a pair of dividers preferably with bows that cannot spring apart. You will need to adapt the dividers to fit a purpose made flat knife edge in the radius arm, and also improvise when cutting these grooves by fitting a temporary block or pad at the centre of radius, i.e. the dial centre.

As mentioned earlier the brass inlay in the original clock is of the 'raised edge' type, but you can fit a flush inlay if you prefer. If brass inlay is not to your liking you could use contrasting strings in maple or other woods, both for the inset strips and also in place of the brass side columns (22) and beaded arch moulding (22).

Completion

Once you have finished the brass inlay woodwork you can then add the remaining clock case fittings, including the stepped base edging, lion's head handles and ball feet. Also make and fit the rear door. The latter is a half jointed assembly with 2mm thick mahogany veneer overlaid to form the internal glazed rebate and the step over the door jamb. With regard to the glass in the rear door, make sure you use 'picture glass' which is thinner than ordinary window glass. This is recommended on all clocks in this book. Finally, fit an eight day movement fixed either to a seatboard or to the case to suit, ensuring the dial plate fits close into the fixed bezel ring (26). Alternatively, the dial plate can be fixed separately into the bezel (26).

PARTS LIST

Item	No	Material	Dimensions (mm)
Casework			
1 Side panel	2	Mahogany	95×7×180 long
2 Case top	1	Mahogany	20×8×1350 long total. Cut and fit in 95 long strips
3 Bottom	1	Mahogany	95×8×150 long
4 Dial board	1	Mahogany	144×10×270 long
5 Base surround	1	Mahogany	24×10×650 long total
6 Side strip	2	Mahogany	16×7×210 long
7 Arch strip	2	Mahogany	30×10×140 total
8 Sill rail	1	Mahogany	30×7×144 long
9 Rear door frame	1	Mahogany	110×7×260 long. Divide into three pieces
10 Door facing strip	1	Mahogany	110×2×260 long. Divide into three pieces
11 Beading	1	Mahogany	5×2.5×1060 long total
12 Support pad	2	Mahogany	8sq×25 total for two
13 Fret back cloth	–	Purple silk	Purchase to suit
14 Veneer	–	Mahogany	Veneer all over case external faces
Glass			
15 Door glass	1	Picture glass	Cut to suit
Metalwork			
16 Hinge	2	Brass	20×7 wide nominal size
17 Lock	1	Brass	Purchase to suit
18 Ball foot	4	Brass	18 dia×13 thick c/w screw fitting
19 Side fret	2	Brass plate	Make from 1mm thick plate. Purchase to suit
20 Lion's head drop ring handle	2	Brass	Purchase to suit
21 Arch moulding strip	1	Brass	Purchase to suit
22 Side column	2	Brass	Purchase to suit

23	Inlay strip	1	Brass	3×1.5 section × 1000 long	26	Dial plate bezel	1	Brass	Purchase to suit dial plate
24	Facing strip	1	Brass	6×0.75 section×600 long	27	Front bezel	1	Brass	Purchase to suit c/w bezel glass
25	Dial plate	1	Enamel plate	114 nominal size	28	Hands	1 pair	Blued steel	Purchase to suit
					29	Movement	1	–	Eight day spring wound c/w pendulum

CHAPTER 6

Balloon clocks

In parallel with the advent of broken arch, round top and lancet style clocks in the late eighteenth century a further type known as the 'balloon clock' also evolved to suit round dials. These were introduced about 1775 and were popular for some 30 years. They have a quite unique style of their own, very different from earlier clock cases with their more regular square shape. Instead the cases have a round top with a narrow curved waist below the dial, spreading out towards a rectanglar base.

Two arguments have been put forward to account for this shape. That most often cited is the pursuit of hot air ballooning invented around 1782, and which progressed greatly in the 25 years following. It is a matter of some conjecture whether horologists noting this development exploited one aspect of their business by making their clocks of similar form. Some authorities suggest that the link is purely hypothetical, though I suspect there may well be an element of truth here somewhere.

On a quite different tack, the other argument for their form is related to the fact that clock makers were slowly discontinuing the use of the verge escapement in bracket clocks, and turning to the more accurate anchor escapement. The pendulum on an anchor escapement has a smaller arc of swing, and this gave more flexibility to adapt case design. Where the balloon clock is waisted below the dial the pendulum swing is quite narrow, and the wider bottom section will accommodate the bob.

Coopered construction

We also see another development in case design which is common to both round top, lancet and balloon clock cases. This is the 'coopered' or

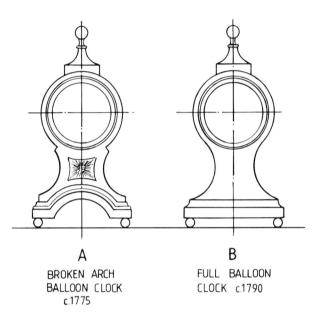

A	B
BROKEN ARCH BALLOON CLOCK c.1775	FULL BALLOON CLOCK c.1790

6.1 *Balloon clock styles*

barrel construction, where the curved top, and in balloon clocks, the case sides as well, are made from narrow strips of wood glued to the edges of the clock front and back panels. These are then smoothed externally to the curved form. To conceal this balloon clocks are always veneered externally.

Most balloon clocks tend to be a little on the tall size typically 450 to 550mm high to suit a dial size of about 200mm. The earliest balloon clocks dating from about 1775 were of the broken arch form as shown in Fig 6.1(A), and incorporated a step in the side below the dial. These tended to have ebonized pear wood cases, and occasionally they were fitted with carrying handles at the side, a legacy from earlier clock case design. By 1790 this clock form had changed in favour of a case without the step as shown in Fig 6.1(B) and cases veneered with mahogany or satinwood predominated.

Balloon clock design

The principal balloon clock design here is from an original thought to date rather later than the general period, at about 1840 as in Fig 6.2. The dial is signed 'Clerke, I.Royal Exchange, London'. The case is of the full balloon form topped by a pyramid crown piece with a ball finial, and stands on matching ball form feet. The fusee compensated movement unusually has a balance wheel escapement.

Construction

The general arrangement is shown in Fig 6.3, and sectional details in Fig 6.4. the dial plate is 195mm O.D. and the minute ring 175mm O.D. If the dial plate/bezel size fitted differs the case outside diameter should be adjusted to suit. Additionally the waist radius could be affected and a small height adjustment may also be necessary. If you wish to make a balloon clock to suit a different dial size, e.g. 150mm, then the case dimensions should be proportionally scaled.

6.2 *Balloon clock*

6.3 (Below) *General arrangement of balloon clock*

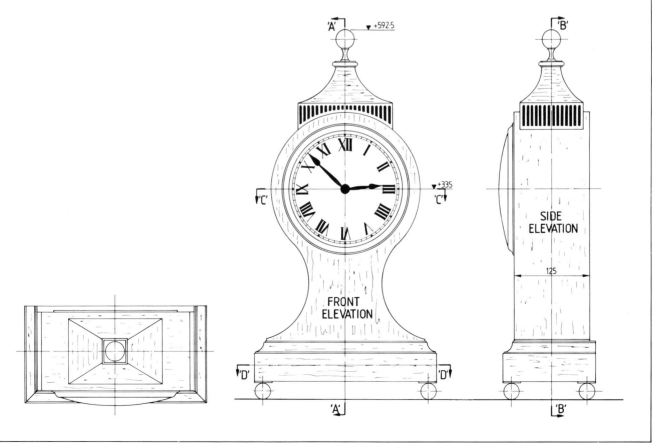

FRONT ELEVATION

SIDE ELEVATION

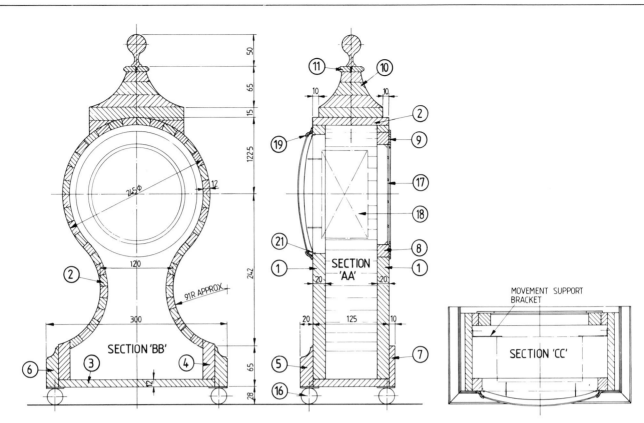

6.4 *Sectional arrangement of balloon clock*

As an alternative to the coopered construction Fig 6.5 shows a glued plywood slab assembly. In this the middle plywood sheets are cut away in the centre to accommodate the clock movement, and lighten the case as much as possible. Although not authentic a plywood case offers a simpler construction if you are not inclined to tackle the coopered design.

6.5 *Rear view and alternative slab construction*

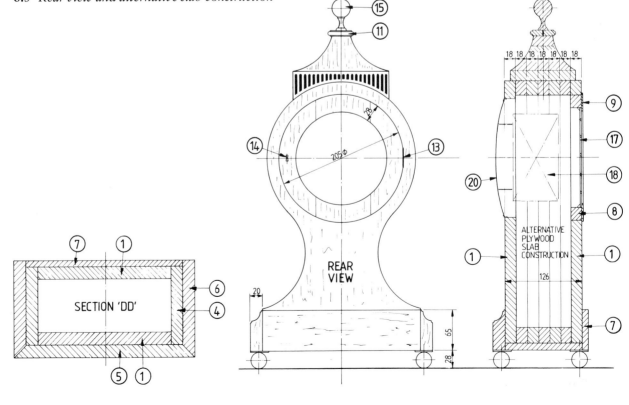

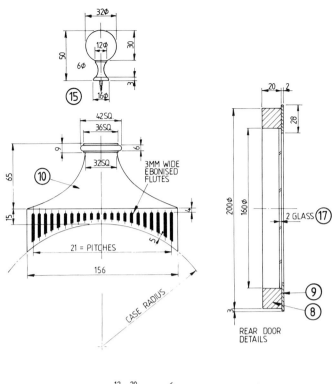

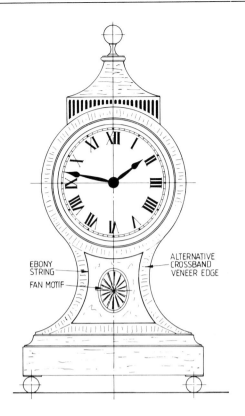

6.7 *Balloon clock with crossbanded veneer edging*

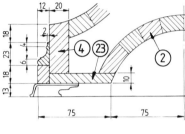

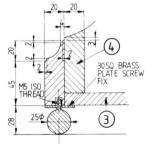

BASE CORNER DETAILS

6.6 *Miscellaneous balloon clock details*

Miscellaneous details

Miscellaneous details of the clock case base construction, crown piece, ball finial and rear door are given in Fig 6.6. Brass ball finials and feet are commercially available though it is equally possible to make these on a metal turning lathe. The crown piece is glued on and screw fixed from the inside of the case. The

original rear door frame is a one piece construction which can be woodturned, but you could economize on wood by using a half jointed framework as in the lancet clock design (Chapter 5). Glue 2mm-thick mahogany on externally to form the glazing rebate and the step across the door jamb. Note that the rear door size must be slightly larger than the dial plate diameter, to give access for inserting the dial plate/movement from behind.

Veneering

In the original clock the veneering is somewhat plain, so as an alternative Fig 6.7 shows what can be done with a little imaginative thinking. This is in the form of additional crossbanding round the dial and case front together with a fan motif. These features were commonly used on early balloon clocks often with contrasting wood veneers. Some clocks also had crossbanding on the case side as well for additional effect.

An important point, if you choose the coopered construction, is to ensure that the veneer grain on the sides runs lengthways, i.e. transverse to the cooper strips. This is to take

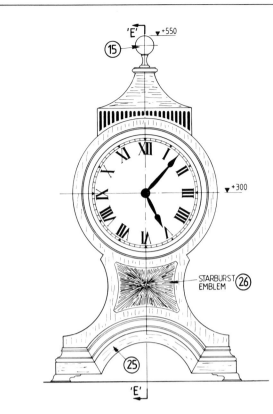

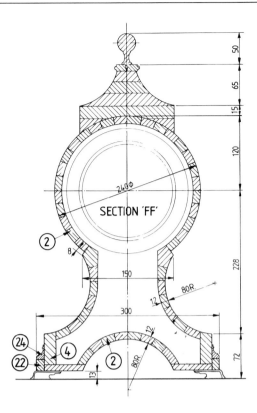

6.8 *General arrangement of broken arch balloon clock*

6.9 (Above & Right) *Sectional arrangement of broken arch bracket clock*

account of wood movement. With a coopered construction there is a tendency for the strips to shrink marginally in width under adverse dry ambient conditions. If the veneer is laid with the grain in the same direction as the sub-structure, any shrinkage which does occur can place stress on the surface veneer which may split under adverse conditions. With a plywood construction however you could veneer either way without adverse effects. You should find that the veneer will flex to the required curvature without further inducement, but a little steaming may help the pieces to retain their form prior to gluing. Veneer the sides before doing the front and back. This way you can use the string and pin technique to hold the side veneer in place while the glue is setting. These pin marks will be later covered over when the front and back face veneers are applied.

Broken arch balloon clocks

Figs 6.8 and 6.9 give details of an alternative broken arch balloon clock design which some may prefer. As mentioned earlier, besides having a base with a broken arch form mirroring the

dial curve, they also have a small step in the case above the waist where it joins the dial. Making a case this way enables you to veneer it in easy steps, with that over the case top being laid separate to the waisted section. Indeed, there is some suggestion that the stepped balloon case was first developed because of limitations in marquetry skill, and that as this improved the case maker was later able to modify this to the full balloon form. The broken arch balloon clock also lends itself to the sunburst emblem which was sometimes used instead of the fan motif.

Movements

Balloon clocks were originally intended to have spring wound movements with pendulum regulation. Broken arch clocks are not so adaptable in this respect, and on early clocks of this style there was often a step in the case behind the front arch so that the pendulum could drop down behind this. Movement suppliers usually quote the pendulum swing overall including the bob size. If difficulty arises it may be possible to fit a smaller bob, or in the

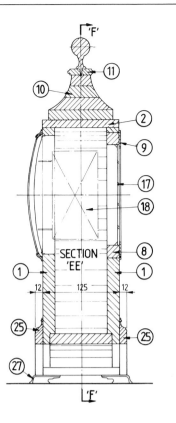

SECTION 'EE'

last resort fit a movement with a balance wheel escapement. Balloon clocks do not have seatboards for practical reasons, and the movement should be bracket fixed to the case.

PARTS LIST

Item	No	Material	Dimensions (mm)
Casework			
1 Front/back	2	Oak	245×20×430 long
2 Cooper strips	–	Oak	20×13×125 long. About 44 required
3 Bottom	1	Oak	125×12×260 long
4 Side strips	2	Oak	65×20×125 long
5 Front rail	1	Oak	65×20×300 long
6 Side rail	2	Oak	65×20×155 long
7 Back rail	1	Oak	65×10×260 long
8 Door frame	1	Mahogany	200×20×200 long
9 Door fascia	1	Mahogany	55×2×600 long
10 Crown piece	1	Oak	105×20×550 long
11 Pad piece	1	Mahogany	42×9×42 long
12 Veneer	–	Mahogany	Veneer externally over all surfaces. Quantity to suit
Metalwork			
13 Door hinge	1	Brass	10×25 long
14 Door lock	1	Brass	Purchase to suit
15 Ball finial	1	Brass	Purchase to suit
16 Ball foot	4	Brass	Purchase to suit
Glass & material			
17 Door glass	1	Picture glass	Cut to suit
Movement			
18 Movement	1	–	Eight day spring wound striking movement
19 Opening bezel	1		Hinged bezel & glass to suit front door, 200 nominal size
20 Dial plate	1	White enamel plate	White dial 200 nominal dia
21 Dial plate bezel			190 nominal diameter
Broken arch balloon clock – alternative			
22 Front/side rail	1	Mahogany	18×12×650 long total
23 Bottom strip	2	Oak	70×10×125 long
24 Rail moulding	1	Mahogany	23×12×700 long total
25 Arch moulding/ rail	2	Mahogany	100×12×220 long
26 Starburst emblem	1	Brass	Purchase to suit
27 Ogee foot	4	Brass	Purchase to suit

CHAPTER 7

Mantel clocks

In the preceding chapters I have featured a number of bracket clocks with dial sizes ranging from 115 (4½in) to 200mm (8in), so by way of a change I will now give details of three small but none the less attractive mantle clocks of the late Victorian and Edwardian period. Two are of balloon form, a revival of the earlier Regency period balloon clocks but in reduced size, and the third is a horizontal style mantel clock. They are all designed to fit insertion movements of nominal size 90mm (3½in). These clocks were made over a long period from the 1870–1920 and some of the best examples have fine marquetry inlay which in some instances is solid silver.

7.1 *Balloon clock (1)*

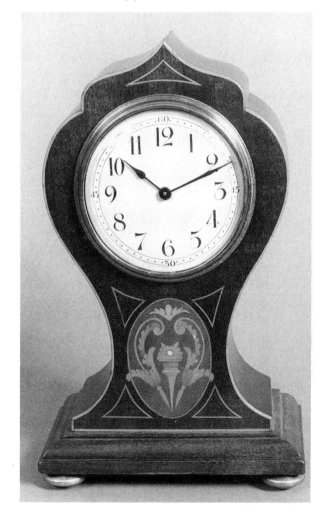

Balloon clock 1

This balloon style Edwardian mantel clock is 248mm (9¾in) high (Fig 7.1). The mahogany case has a curved pointed top with re-entrant style corners, and a narrow waisted section below the dial over a moulded rectangular base. The convex dial with a fixed bezel features fine calligraphic arabic numerals, a minute ring with divisions marked in small spots, and spade style hands. The insertion movement fits in a brass lined hole through the case. Access for winding is from behind via a removable pressed backplate. The front of the case is edged and inset with contrasting pale wood strings, and in the waisted section there is an elliptical marquetry motif. The clock stands on pressed brass button feet.

Construction

The general arrangement drawings are given in Fig 7.2 and sectional details in Fig 7.3. Construction is relatively simple and I do not propose to discuss this in any great detail. Regarding the case, you can bandsaw this externally to shape and drill out the waste material in the centre ready for the insertion movement. To finish curved sawn surfaces by hand is never the easiest job particularly for the more difficult concave surfaces as on this clock. A very useful tool for doing this is a drum sander attachment for the drill press. You can also use this to clean up the insertion movement hole after drilling out the waste material. An alternative way of cleaning up concave surfaces is to use a shaped sanding pad. Make sure the pointed top and the re-entrant corners are nice and clean. Lastly cut and fit the inlay strings and carefully execute the marquety oval. On the original clock these strings are of a contrasting pale wood such as maple or sycamore. Inlay techniques are briefly discussed in Chapter 5. Finally clean up and French polish the case.

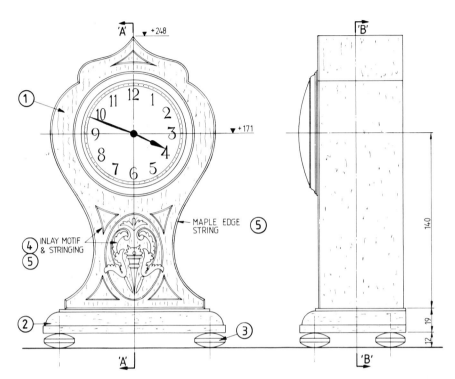

7.2 *General arrangement of balloon clock (1)*

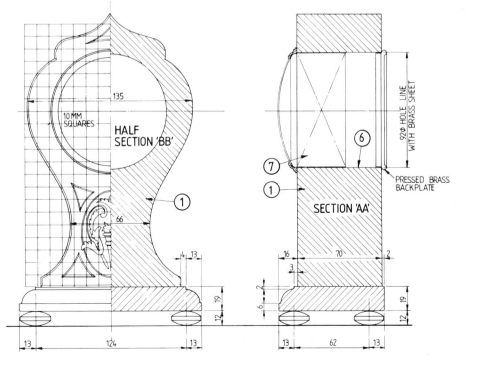

7.2 *Sectional arrangement of balloon clock (1)*

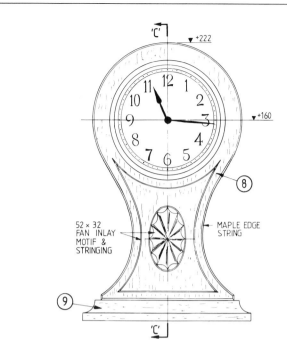

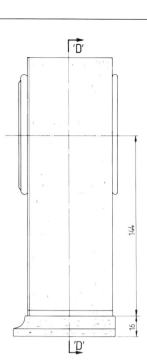

7.5 *General arrangement of balloon clock (2)*

7.4 *Balloon clock (2)*

Insertion movement

Obtaining a suitable insertion movement can give problems. Supplier sources are given in the appendix, but availability does vary among manufacturers and you may have to search around a bit to find what you want. To be authentic a spring wound movement really ought to be fitted, but insertion movements today mostly seem to be quartz so there may be little or no choice. Insertion movements for small mantle clocks vary between 70mm (2¾in) and 115mm (4½in) diameter. If you are unable to find one of the size quoted you should consider scaling the case up or down to suit. The brass lining for the insertion movement is an optional fitment. The original button feet are made from pressed brass sheet and not easy to come by. These could be machined from the solid on a metal turning lathe if you have one available. Alternatively brass ball caddy feet which are commercially available, and are suited to the design, could be fitted.

Balloon clock 2

This mahogany case Edwardian mantle clock is 222mm (8¾in) high and is of the true balloon

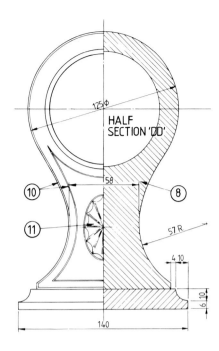

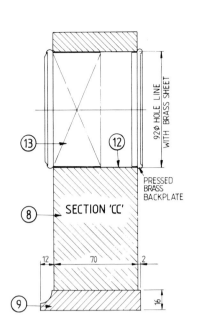

7.6 *Sectional arrangement of balloon clock (2)*

style with a curved waisted section below the dial over a moulded rectangular base (Fig 7.4). The dial features arabic numerals, a diamond marked minute ring, and spade style hands as balloon clock 1, but with a bevelled flat glass bezel. The rear wound insertion movement has a platform escapement and fits in a brass lined hole fitted with a pressed brass backplate. The case front is edged and inset with pale wood strings, and has a simple sand shaded fan marquetry motif below the dial. The base has a cove shaped edge.

Construction

The general arrangement is shown in Fig 7.5 and sectional details in Fig 7.6. The construction is similar to balloon clock 1 (see p. 48).

Mantel clock 3

The third timepiece is a horizontal style mantel clock dating about 1870 (Fig 7.7). This clock case is veneered in burr walnut veneer over a pinewood base. The insertion movement fits into a circular case surround cradled in a curved support, which sits onto a base consisting of an ebonized cove moulding over a rectangular

7.7 *Mantel clock (3)*

frame bottom. The case is decorated with two ebonized roundels below the dial which is signed 'Hry Marc, Paris'.

The eight day French movement has a deadbeat escapement and is inscribed on the backplate 'VAP Brevete SCOC'. The letters VAP are the initials of the clock maker Victor-Athansase-Pierret (1806–1893). The flat white dial features finely detailed Roman numerals, a minute ring with spotted five minute markings, and moon style hands. Inside the pressed brass backplate is the original note with instructions on how to set the clock reading as follows:

'8 day timepiece dead beat escapement setting itself in beat with a good shake to give impulsion to the pendulum. Wind up to the left. The small square in the centre is to set the hands. To regulate it turn the pendulum ball to the left when it gains and to the right when it loses'.

7.8 Mantel clock movement

7.9 Mantel clock instructions

Construction

First woodturn the case (14) to suit the insertion movement. Use a bandsaw to cut the cradle (15) to size and finish using the drum sanding techniques mentioned earlier. Cut the base strip (17) and half joint this together as shown in section GG, then strengthen this with additional corner strips (18) glued to place. Cut the moulding strip (16) profile with a router, and mitre and glue this together to fit onto the base frame. After cleaning up, ebonize the moulding strip externally.

Polished ebonized surfaces should not show any grain after finishing. The procedure for this is first to black stain the surface, then to seal the grain with a shellac base sealer and lastly to French polish the item. To achieve the grainless intense black finish add spirit black to the French polish.

Before gluing together the final assembly apply the burr walnut veneer to the case (14), cradle (15) and base frame (17). The curvature of the case (14) and the brittle nature of burr walnut is such that some steaming assistance may be required to bend the veneer to the case profile. You can either turn the roundels (19) from real ebony or alternatively use pear and wood and ebonize these as discussed above. They are shown with a back spigot but this is optional. An alternative is to paper glue the blanks for these to the faceplate prior to turning.

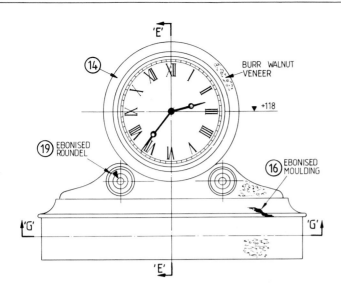

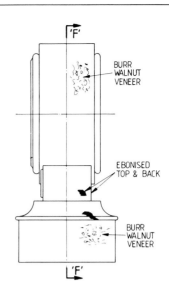

MANTEL CLOCK

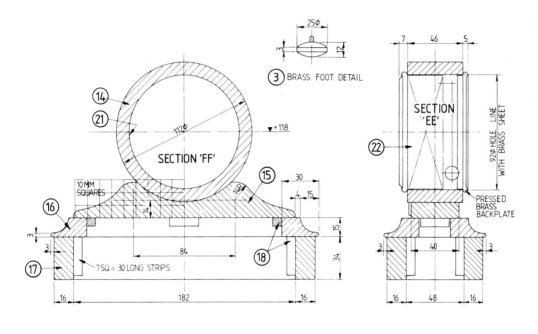

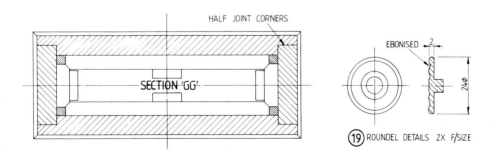

7.10 *General arrangement and sections of mantel clock*

PARTS LIST

Item	No	Material	Dimensions (mm)

Balloon clock 1

Item	No	Material	Dimensions (mm)
1 Case	1	Mahogany	135×70×220 long
2 Base	1	Mahogany	88×19×150 long
3 Foot	4	Brass	Purchase or make to suit
4 Inlay string	–	Maple	Purchase to suit
5 Inlay motif	1		Make to details shown on drawing. Use contrasting woods for effect
6 Lining	1	Brass	300×70 sheet of thin gauge brass. Bend to suit
7 Movement	1		90 O.D. spring wound insertion movement c/w pressed brass backplate

Balloon clock 2

Item	No	Material	Dimensions (mm)
8 Case	1	Mahogany	120×70×210 long
9 Base	1	Mahogany	84×16×140 long
10 Inlay string	–	Maple	Purchase to suit
11 Fan motif	1	–	Purchase or make to suit
12 Lining	1	Brass	300×70 sheet of thin gauge brass. Bend to suit
13 Movement	1		90 O.D. spring wound insertion movement c/w pressed brass backplate

Mantel clock 3

Item	No	Material	Dimensions (mm)
14 Case	1	Pine	120×50×120 long
15 Cradle	1	Pine	40×32×190 long
16 Moulding strip	1	Pine	30×15×650 long total
17 Base strip	1	Pine	34×16×600 long total
18 Support strip	1	Pine	7sq×220 long total
19 Roundel	2	Pine	30×10×30 long
20 Veneer	1	Walnut	Burr walnut veneer all over except where indicated
21 Lining	1	Brass	300×70 piece of thin gauge brass sheet. Bend to suit
22 Movement	1	–	90 O.D. spring wound insertion movement c/w pressed brass backplate

WALL
CLOCKS

CHAPTER 8

Nine-light Viennese regulator

Vienna regulators

In the Biedermeier period (1810–1850) there existed in Vienna a group of clock makers who were producing clocks of extremely high quality both in the movement and in the style of case. These clocks, termed Vienna regulators, were precision timepieces and were characterized by high quality weight driven movements, dead beat escapements, fine wheel work, one piece dials with engine turned bezels, and steel rod pendulums. The more expensive clocks were fitted with extra features such as maintaining power, a grand-sonnerie strike (Viennese 4/4 strike), night silencing and a repeat facility. They ran typically for eight days, but finer examples were month, three months or even year going. The Laterndluhr (lantern) style cases too were of extremely fine proportions, with slim framing and large glazed panels on all sides to display the movement to the maximum advantage.

Nine-light Laterndluhr

The nine-light Laterndluhr Vienna regulator probably evolved from an earlier Empire style case as shown in Fig 8.1. The nine-light case (nine glazed panels) has a hood section with an architectural top housing the dial and movement, a narrower trunk and a box enclosure for the pendulum. The cases were made from stable straight grained pine, veneered internally and externally with choice timbers such as mahogany, rosewood, walnut, ash and fruitwoods.

All the glazed panels were outlined in a constrasting wood such as maple and the arched trunk door had characteristic maple strings to

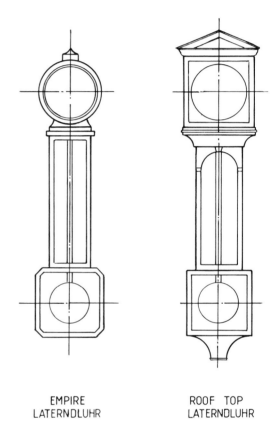

EMPIRE
LATERNDLUHR

ROOF TOP
LATERNDLUHR

8.1 *Laterndluhr clock styles*

the top and side. The doors were often sliding rather than hinged. The earliest Laterndluhr clocks had roof mouldings which were of smaller section than on later cases, and the concave moulding on the trunk beneath the hood was only on the sides and did not extend to the front.

These cases consequently have a flat unstepped profile when viewed from the side. Laterndluhr clocks are much sought after because of their rarity, elegance and simplicity.

Case design

The clock design is based upon a nine-light Laterndluhr Vienna regulator that I was fortunate to get the opportunity to measure prior to restoration. I had waited patiently for this to come into England from Budapest. There was a problem, though, which I had not predicted: this was the pendulum length of 700mm (28in), and I knew immediately that it would not be easy to find a commercial movement today to suit this. The closest movements available are either seconds beat (994mm) or three quarter seconds (559mm) and clearly a 700mm pendulum fell neatly in between! Nine-light Laterndluhr clocks were made with seconds pendulums, so I finally decided to scale the measurements up to suit, and fit the case round a larger 240mm O.D. dial plate. The drawings shown are proportionally a very good match to the original clock measured.

The original nine-light Laterndluhr clock dates between 1830–35 and is typical of the Biedermeier period. It has an eight day movement with a dead beat escapement, a steel pendulum with a brass bob, and a grand-sonnerie strike/repeat facility. The going train is weight driven and for the strike there are two spring wound barrels. The dial plate is signed 'Seif in Wien' and has an engine turned bezel. The case is mahogany veneered over a pine base and has nine glazed panels giving maximum visibility to the movement on all sides. Access to the movement is via a removable hood section, and for winding by a hinged hood door. Further sliding style access doors are fitted to the trunk and the pendulum box. The trunk door has a square top and the glazed side panels are outlined with maple strings.

Construction

The general arrangement is given in Fig 8.3 and principal sections in Fig 8.4. Enlarged views of the hood and pendulum box are shown in Fig 8.5. Cross sections through the case at various levels are given in Figs 8.6 and 8.7. The case construction is in two parts comprising the hood and the trunk/pendulum box. The hood design is based on a dial bezel O.D. of 240mm. If the dial size fitted varies from this you should make proportional adjustments to the casework to suit. The case is designed to house a seconds

8.2 Nine-light Laterndluhr clock

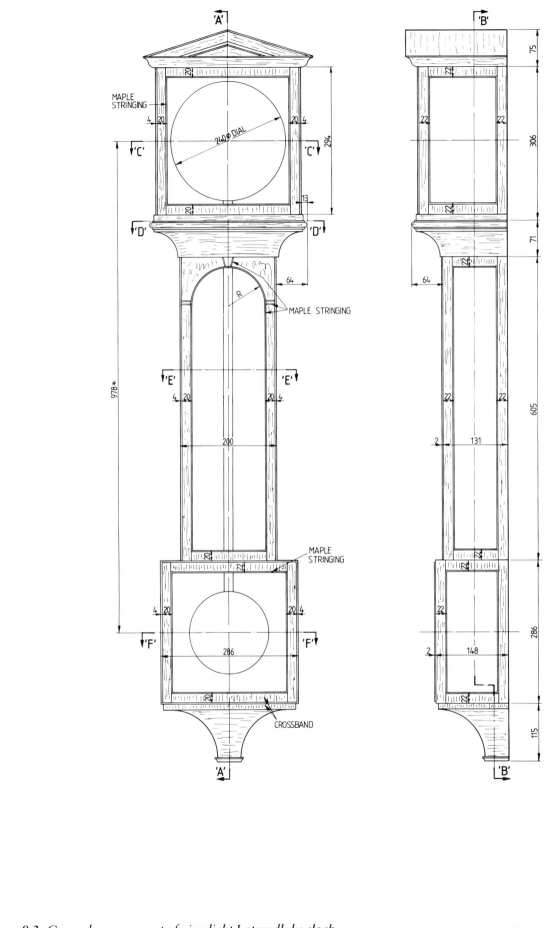

8.3 *General arrangement of nine-light Laterndluhr clock*

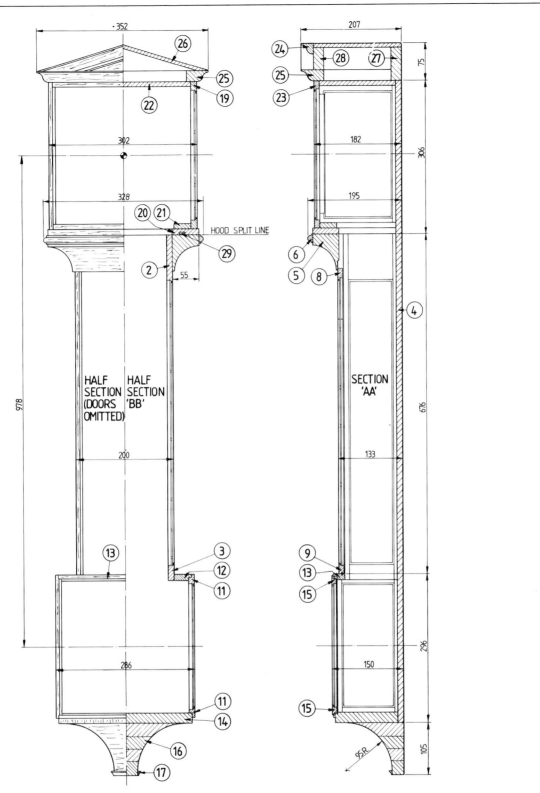

8.4 *Sectional arrangement of nine-light Laterndluhr clock*

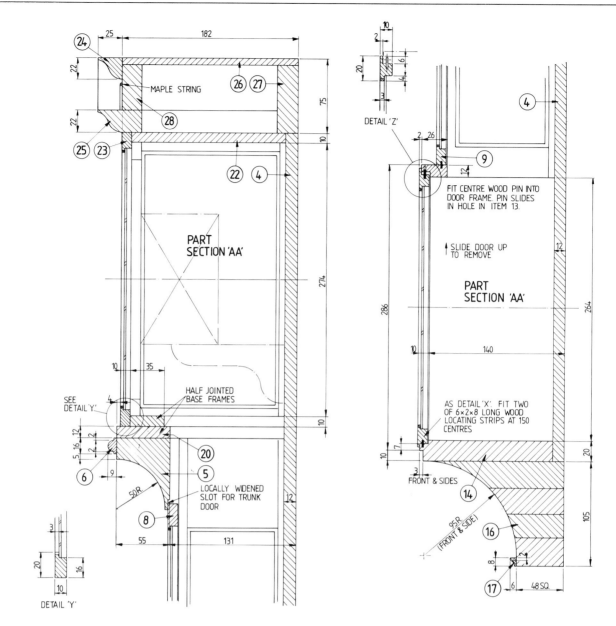

8.5 *Hood and base sections*

Trunk/pendulum box

pendulum with an overall swing of 270mm (preferably less) using a 165mm O.D. brass bob. The pendulum box in particular is necessarily closely fitted to the pendulum bob for aesthetic reasons. Check the case measurements carefully with the proposed movement and make adjustments if necessary before proceeding. When the movement is available rig it up temporarily on a board to ensure the pendulum swing is within the limits prescribed.

Trunk/pendulum box

The construction of the trunk and pendulum box can be split into a number of items. These

are the trunk and pendulum box sidelight frames, the pendant, the back, and the sliding doors.

Sidelights

Commence construction by making the trunk sidelights consist of items (1), (2) and (3) which are half jointed. Rebate these frames internally to fit the glass, and also on the front and back edges to fit the trunk door and the back panel (4). On the original case the sidelights are of straight grained pine with mahogany veneering both internally and externally. If you wish to be authentic this is the way to do it, but as an

60

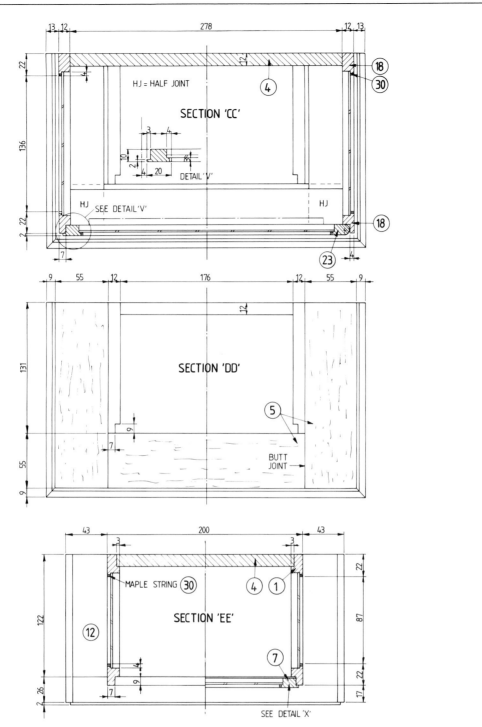

8.6 *Casework cross sections (1)*

alternative you could save some work by making the sidelights from solid mahogany with external veneering only. The latter is necessary to accommodate the crossbanding on the top and bottom rails. Finish the frames by adding the maple outlining strings.

The pendulum box sidelights comprise items (10) and (11) and you construct these in a similar manner to the trunk sidelights. Note that the rails need additional rebating (11) on the top and bottom edges to fit the side strips (12) and the pendulum box bottom (14).

Pendant

The pendant is a glued sandwich construction consisting of items (14), (16) and (17). Carefully

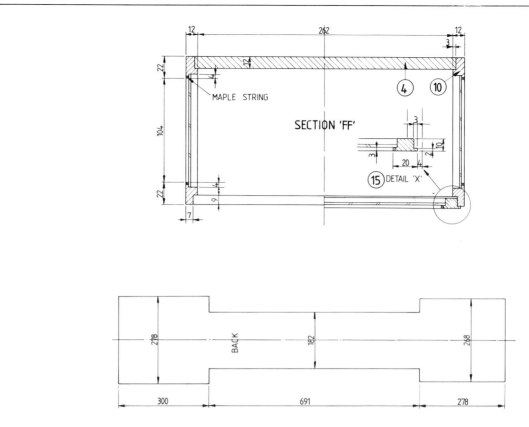

8.7 *Casework cross sections (2)*

mark out the profile and after cutting and gluing, sand the surface smooth surface for veneering. Complete the mahogany veneering on the pendant prior to assembly, including the crossbanding round the edge of item (14). The veneer should fit the curvature without the need for steaming. The beading (17) is a small coving and you should fit a contrasting maple string round the edge.

Assembly

Once you have completed the principal case components you can proceed, lastly, to make the back (4) to details as in Fig 8.6. Veneer this with mahogany on the front and add a balancing veneer behind to prevent warping. Then carry out a trial assembly to make sure the components all fit neatly together, and add the side rails (12), and the bridge rail (13) to stabilize the pendulum box assembly. Take the opportunity to do some prepolishing work prior to gluing which is easier on the loose components. When the fit is satisfactory glue and cramp the assembly and leave aside to set.

Trunk top moulding

Dimensional details of the trunk top mouldings items (5) and (6) are given in Fig 8.5. You can machine the torus moulding (6) with a router, but the larger moulding (5) is probably outside the range of a normal hand router, so you may have to work this by hand. You can make this easier by removing some of the waste material on the circular saw. If you make it this way use a card or perspex pattern to check the curved profile and a rule for the straightness. Before gluing the moulding (5) to the trunk make sure the front piece is suitably rebated at the back so that the trunk door can slide up behind it. Also, check that the trunk width is parallel top and bottom. Lastly, veneer the moulding (5) externally.

Hood

The hood casework consists of two sidelight frames, a base framework, a top panel, a pivoted door, and an architectural roof style top. Make the sidelights (18, 19), rebating and veneering these similar to the other sidelights as described above. Also make the base framework (20) using half joint connections at the corners. Glue stiffening strips (21) onto this to locate the sidelights and to act as a door stop at the front. The architectural top consists of items (24) to (28) which you should machine and cut to the details given. Mitre the ogee frame (25) and glue this to the top panel (22), and then add the other components to suit. The fascia strip (28) is mahogany veneered on the front and has an applied maple string (see Fig 8.5). You should complete this veneer work before gluing the roof unit together. With the principal components finished you can then attempt a trial assembly of the hood. When you glue and cramp it together make sure the hood is square to accept the door fitted later. It may help to fix a diagonal strip temporarily across the back during the gluing operation to set this.

Hood/trunk fitting

On the original the hood slides on to the top of the trunk section via dovetail strips (29). A simpler method of fixing this is to extend the trunk sidelight frames up to the level of the top of the base frame (20), and glue on a flat strip overlapping the edge of the base frame. The extended frames act as guides and the lap strip prevents the hood from being accidentally dislodged.

Doors

The clock has three access doors. Those on the trunk and pendulum box are sliding frames and that on the hood hinges on pivot plates. You construct these similar to the sidelights detailed earlier using half joint connections at the corners. Note especially the veneer crossbanding on these doors, also the angled maple strings fitted at the top of the trunk door arch and the two short strings either side, which is characteristic of the period these clocks were made. The method of fixing the doors is as follows.

The pendulum box door frame has two small wooden locating tongues glued into the bottom rail, and a further wooden pin fixed into the top rail. The top pin fits into a small hole drilled in the bridge rail (13) and the tongue pieces fit into two matching slots cut into the case bottom (14). You fit the door by first positioning it into the recess via the top pin, lifting it so the tongue pieces clear the case bottom, and then move the frame in so the tongues drop into the bottom slots. To make this work you must ensure there is sufficient vertical clearance in the framework to permit this sliding movement (see Fig 8.5 detail 'Z'). You locate the trunk door in a similar way except that at the top the frame slides up behind the trunk top moulding (5).

Hinging the hood doors poses a different problem, for on the original there was no visible evidence as to how the pivot pins had been got in. Fortunately there is an easy solution which is to hinge this in the manner hood doors are hung on longcase clocks. To do this make two small pivot plate hinges, each consisting of a 9 by 30mm long brass plate with a short 2mm diameter brass pivot pin brazed into one end. To fix the hood door in place first offer the brass plate pins into pivot holes drilled into the top and bottom edges of the hood door frame. Then slide the door into position in the hood and screw fix the plates into the edges of items (20, 22).

Movement and dial

As mentioned earlier there are very few dials and movements of a suitable quality to match such a fine case. The proposed movement is a Kieninger 10240 RWS with a seconds beat white wood pendulum, 165mm brass bob, and a 240mm O.D. flat white dial. By diligent searching you may find other alternatives. The important thing to remember is always to fit a one piece flat dial plate. Two piece Vienna dial plates introduced rather later in the nineteenth century would be totally out of character for a Laterndluhr style clock. Also if you can fit a steel pendulum rod instead of a white wood one this would be more periodically correct.

PARTS LIST

Item	No	Material	Dimensions (mm)
Trunk			
1 Trunk sidelight stile	4	Pine	20×12×688 long
2 Trunk sidelight top rail	2	Pine	91×12×131 long
3 Trunk sidelight bottom rail	2	Pine	32×12×131 long
4 Back	1	Pine	278×12×1268 long
5 Trunk top moulding	1	Pine	71×55×750 long total
6 Torus edge moulding	1	Mahogany	16×9×750 long total
7 Trunk door stile	2	Mahogany	20×10×610 long
8 Trunk door top rail	1	Mahogany	121×10×196 long
9 Trunk door bottom rail	2	Mahogany	20×10×196 long
Pendulum box			
10 Sidelight stile (2)	4	Pine	22×12×286 long
11 Sidelight rail (2)	4	Pine	22×12×148 long
12 Side strip	2	Pine	37×12×148 long
13 Bridge rail	1	Mahogany	26×12×286 long
14 Pendulum box base	1	Pine	136×20×278 long
15 Pendulum box door rail	4	Mahogany	20×10×278 long
16 Pendant block	1	Pine	150×30×400 long total
17 Pendant moulding	1	Mahogany	8×6×150 long total
Hood			
18 Hood sidelight stile	4	Pine	22×12×306 long
19 Hood sidelight rail	4	Pine	22×12×180 long
20 Hood base frame strip	1	Pine	55×12×700 long total. Cut into three & half joint together
21 Stiffening strip	1	Pine	35×10×620 long total
22 Hood top panel	1	Pine	160×10×278 long
23 Hood door rail	4	Mahogany	20×10×294 long
24 Roof ogee moulding (1)	1	Mahogany	25×22×400 long
25 Roof ogee moulding (2)	1	Mahogany	47×22×800 long
26 Roof panel	2	Pine	182×7×200 long
27 Roof back strip	1	Pine	68×22×320 long
28 Roof fascia strip	1	Pine	46×22×320 long
29 Dovetail slide strip	2	Pine	13×6×160 long
30 Veneer & stringing	–	Mahogany & maple	Mahogany veneer external & interior case, maple string round interior edges of doors & sidelights
Glass			
31 Glass	–	Picture glass	Cut to suit doors & sidelights
Movement			
32 Movement	1		10240 RSW Kieninger eight day Vienna regulator c/w 240 dia white dial & seconds pendulum (165mm bob)

Daniel Quare bracket clock (c.1690)

Lancet bracket clock (c.1800)

Balloon style Edwardian mantel clock

Vienna Regulator (c.1880)

Round dial tavern clock

Black Forest wall clock (c.1880)

Cuckoo clock

Marquetry longcase clock (c.1685)

Detail of case on marquetry longcase clock

CHAPTER 9

Vienna regulator

(c. 1880)

The Vienna regulator which most people are probably familiar with is the later 1880s style wall clock as shown in Fig 9.1. The title is really a misnomer, though, for they are not true 'regulators' in the sense of being finely built timepieces, neither did the vast majority originate from Vienna. However, the name seems to have stuck and this is the title by which we refer to these clocks today. These 'factory clocks' were glazed on three sides to display the movement to the maximum advantage, and typically had either mahogany or walnut casework with contrasting ebonized features. Split turnings were often applied to the cases and there was usually a carved figurehead on the crest. Most originate from either Austria or Germany, and the movements are generally of good quality.

Case description

The Vienna regulator here has glazed panels to the front and sides, with a crestwork panel above the dial and a pendant section below. The casework is mahogany and the glazed door giving access for winding has contrasting ebonized side columns with fluted sections top and bottom. The crest panel and pendant feature ebonized finials and spindles, and there is a carved figurehead in the middle above the dial. The 'Vienna' movement is eight day spring wound regulated by a half seconds pendulum and the bob is marked 'R/A'. This marking, often seen on Vienna wall clocks, is an abbreviation for 'retard/advance', the adjustment being by the pendulum rating nut below. The enamelled dial plate is of two piece construction with an inner brass zone, and the

9.1 *Vienna regulator*

hands are of unusually fine quality. The clock is signed 'Otto Pohland, Chemitz' on the beat plaque. Chemitz is a town west of Dresden in Germany renamed 'Karl-Marx-Stadt' during the Cold War.

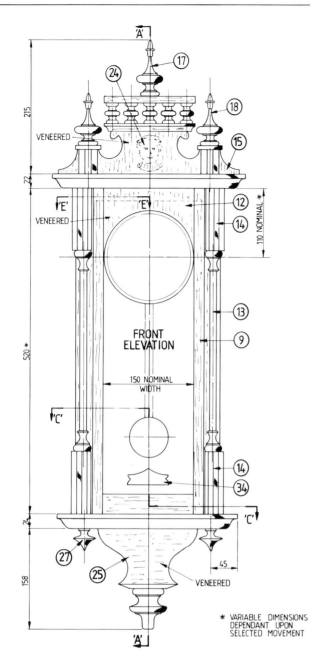

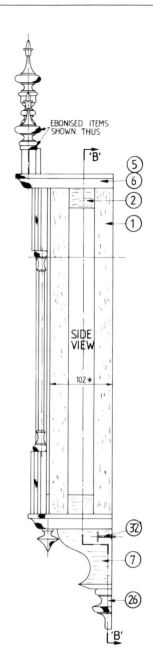

9.4 *General arrangement of Vienna regulator*

9.2 *Crestwork*

9.3 *Pendant*

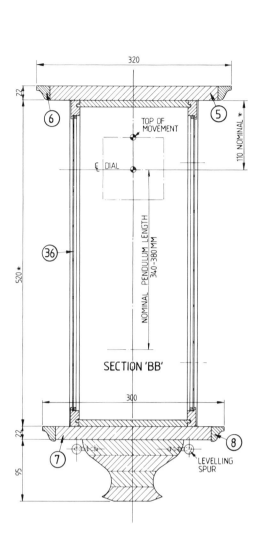

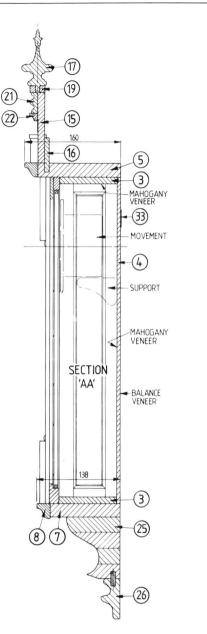

9.5 *Sectional arrangement of Vienna regulator*

Construction

The general arrangement is shown in Fig 9.4 with principal sections in Fig 9.5. Dimensions of the crestwork and pendant are given in Fig 9.6. Enlarged casework details are shown in Fig 9.7 as are finial and columns. The design is based on a dial plate nominally 150mm O.D. over the bezel. If the dial size fitted differs from this you may need to adjust the case width. The case depth could also be affected by the movement selected. The construction is in three parts, the case, the crestwork and the pendant.

Case

The case comprises the sidelights, top and bottom (3) and the back (4). The sidelights are simple frames half jointed at the corners and rebated internally to suit the glazing. In the parts list these are quoted as solid mahogany, but it was common for the sidelight rebate construction on Viennese clocks to be made in thick mahogany (or walnut) veneer over a pine frame, with the internal visible softwood having a simulated finish to suit. I have offered the solid construction as an alternative, but you could do

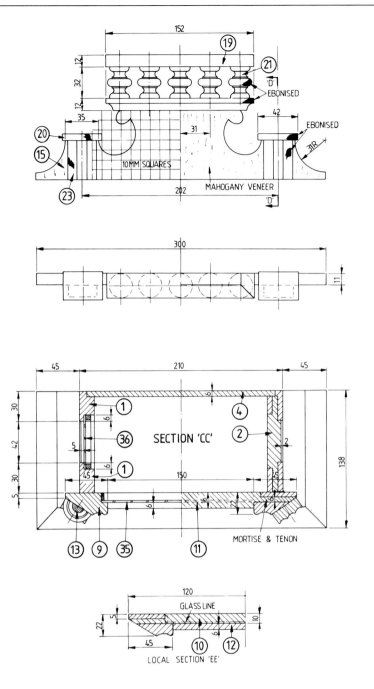

9.6 *Crestwork and casework cross section*

it either way. Next make the top and bottom (3) and tongue joint this into the sides, then move on to make the back (4). The original back was pine, but you could use plywood which offers more stability against warping though less authentic. Veneer this prior to fixing it to the case. With the above items completed carry out a trial assembly of the case and when satisfactory glue fix this. I suggest that you apply

the finish (e.g. French polishing), to the sidelights, and back as work progresses as access problems generally make this more difficult to do later. Lastly prepare the crest and pendant boards (5) and (7) together with the moulded edges (6) and (8), and glue fix these to the case top and bottom respectively. Finish the top side of the crest board (5) and the underside of the pendant board (7) with a matt black paint.

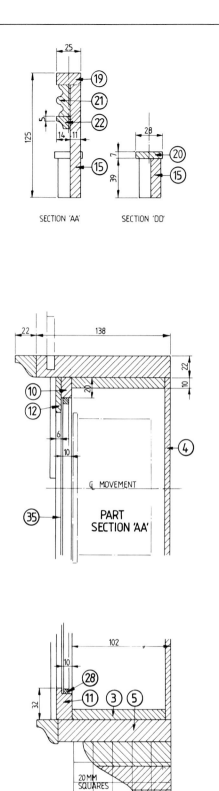

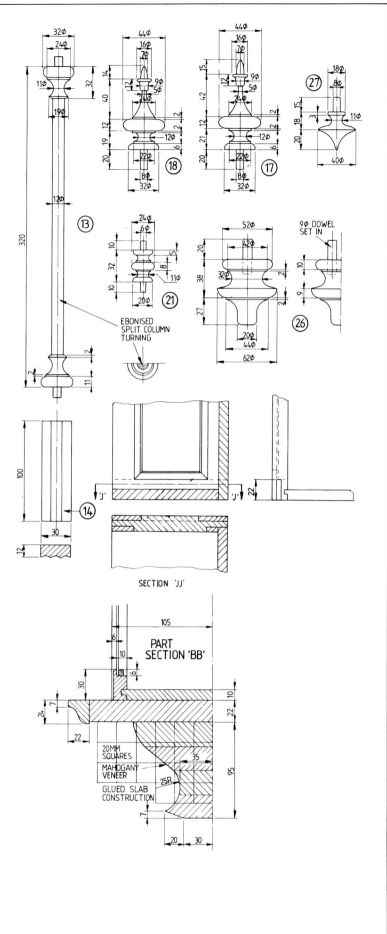

9.7 *Casework, column and finial details*

Crestwork

The crestwork is a loose item which is pegged into a mortice slot in the top of the roof board (5). It consists of a panel (15) which you should first veneer with mahogany, and then add on the various mouldings, strips and finals. The fluted moulding (23) is of similar section and profile to that on the door column item (14). Prepare this in one long length and divided it up as necessary to suit. You could employ routing techniques to make this, or alternatively use a scratch stock with a rounded sanding block for finishing. The method of making the split spindles (21) used on the crest is described below.

Pendant

The pendant is of glued slab construction shaped to the profile shown in Fig 9.7 and is veneered externally. Use a drum sander for finishing the concave surfaces. If you lay the veneer horizontally as on the original, you should be able to bend this to the profile shown without special inducement. If trouble is experienced damp this with hot water and clamp with cauls while drying off, and then glue fix. Finally glue fix the finished pendant to the pendant board (7).

Split turned items

You make each of the split columns (13), crest spindles (21), and pendant finial (26), by woodturning two half strips of wood fixed together with scotch glue. After machining these on the lathe separate them by soaking in water. The method is described in more detail in Chapter 15 (barley twist columns) along with the precautions necessary. You may need a lathe steady to turn the columns (13) which are long and slender. It is easier if you turn the finials (21) in a group rather than individually, and then divide and split them to suit.

Door

Make the access door using a half jointed construction similar to the sidelights. Although it is shown as one piece, you could make the bottom door rail (11) in two parts similar to the top of the frame, i.e. with a 6mm thick mahogany strip applied over a 10mm thick bottom rail. Strengthen the assembly by fixing on the dial mask (12) and then finish the door by adding the flute end pieces (14) and split columns (13). Finally cut and fix the glazing. Mount the door on side pattern hinges and add a small brass hook and eye to latch it shut.

Ebonizing

It is generally very difficult to ebonize mouldings, split turned items and finials *in situ* without first masking and taking care to avoid the finish spilling over to other areas. Conversely, it is equally difficult to finish the mahogany/walnut casework without screening the ebonized items in a similar manner. It is therefore better if you pre-finish the ebonized parts before fixing them to the casework, and it helps if the latter is polished beforehand. An ebonized finish should ideally completely conceal the wood grain, but this is often difficult to achieve because in the polishing process the black stain is sometimes penetrated. It tends to be particularly troublesome on the corners and on turned items.

There are three aspects to successful ebonizing: the wood, the stain and the finish. First, not all woods are suited to ebonizing. The better ones are close grained woods such as apple, pear, holly and cherry. Mahogany will also ebonize but needs more grain filling than the others. I have mentioned before that early English bracket clocks with ebonized cases were often made of pear because it was ideally suited for this, e.g. the Daniel Quare bracket clock in Chapter 2. In the parts list ebonized parts are shown as pear, this being the preferred choice rather than perhaps what the original parts were made of. Second, if you are French polishing use an oil based stain as spirit stains tend to be more difficult to use. Third, when bodying up add spirit black to the French polish. As the finish is built up this will then achieve the intense black that is needed. If at the end there are still problem areas you can touch these in with a small brush. Handle the ebonized items carefully when you fix them to the case, use the minimum of glue to hold them and carefully clean off any excess. Tie the casework round with string or straps to hold the spindles and columns in close contact with the surface while the glue is setting.

For a more comprehensive treatise on ebonizing see Frederick Oughton's book on Wood Finishing (see Further reading).

Movement and dial

Fit the clock with an eight day spring wound movement having a 150mm O.D. enamel finish dial plate with a brass zone and brass ring. Vienna style movements are normally mounted on brackets screwed to the back of the case. On larger wall clocks the pendulum is often mounted separately from the movement on a cock plate fixed to the back and drives the pendulum through a crutch.

On small Vienna wall clocks like this one the pendulum may well be mounted on a cock plate fixed to the movement. The hour strike on Vienna regulators is typically on a spiral gong, with the chime if provided being on a row of rod gongs. This compares with English bracket and longcase clocks which normally strike on a bell.

PARTS LIST

Item	No	Material	Dimensions (mm)
Casework			
1 Sidelight stile	4	Mahogany	30×16×520 long
2 Sidelight rail	4	Mahogany	30×16×102 long
3 Top/ bottom board	2	Mahogany	102×10×210 long
4 Backboard	1	Pine	200×10×520 long
5 Crest board	1	Pine	138×22×276 long
6 Edge moulding (1)	1	Pear	22sq×660 long total
7 Pendant board	1	Pine	116×22×256 long total
8 Edge moulding (2)	1	Pear	24×22×600 long total
9 Door stile	2	Mahogany	45×22×520 long
10 Door top rail	1	Mahogany	20×16×240 long
11 Door bottom rail	1	Mahogany	32×16×240 long
12 Dial mask	1	Mahogany	150×6×110 long
13 Door column	2	Pear	40×20×350 long – see notes on split turning
14 Column flute piece	4	Pear	30×12×100 long
15 Crest panel	1	Pine	113×11×300 long
16 Support strip	1	Pine	45×8×60 long
17 Crest top finial	1	Pear	50sq×120 long
18 Crest side finial	2	Pear	50sq×115 long
19 Finial plinth (1)	1	Pine	25×12×152 long
20 Finial plinth (2)	2	Pear	28×7×42 long
21 Crest spindle	2	Pear	30×15×150 long – see notes on split turning
22 Crest edge moulding	1	Pear	14×12×220 long
23 Crest flute moulding	2	Pear	30×12×39 long
24 Figurehead	1	–	Purchase to suit
25 Pendant	1	Pine	90×25×900 long total. Glued slab construction
26 Pendant finial	1	Pear	65sq×90 long
27 Bottom finial	2	Pear	44sq×70 long
28 Beading	1	Mahogany	6sq×3500 long total
29 Veneer	–	Mahogany	Purchase to suit
Metalwork			
30 Hinge	2	Brass	10 wide×25 long
31 Door catch	1	Brass	Purchase to suit
32 Levelling spur	2	Brass	Purchase to suit
33 Wall plate	1	Brass	Purchase to suit

34	Beat plaque	1	Enamelled plate	Purchase to suit
35	Door glass	1	Picture glass	480×164
36	Sidelight glass	2	Picture glass	472×54

Glass

(see above)

Movement

| 37 | Movement | 1 | – | Spring wound eight day Vienna regulator c/w dial O.D. 150 & pendulum |

CHAPTER 10

Black dial clock

(c.1760)

In the next three chapters I will be looking at the design of English dial clocks over the period 1700–1900. Fig 10.1 illustrates the changes in style which occurred over this time. The earliest black dial clocks (A) had gold numerals and salt box style cases and date from about 1760. The rather larger tavern clock (B) was made for about a 120 years from 1720 onwards and the black shield pattern is a typical mid-century design. The so-called 'cartel' clock (C) with its carved gilded surround made a brief appearance, but quickly gave way to the round white dial clock which was produced in large numbers and survived from about 1770 through to about 1920. The earliest white dials clocks retained the salt box case style but the dial surrounds were much narrower than their black dial counterparts. Later the casework lost the salt

box style projections, and the bottom became rounded instead of square as in (D). In the 'drop box' dial clock (E) the case was extended below the dial to house a longer pendulum. The dial surrounds on early white dials clocks (1770–1810) had a narrow concave profile but after this the convex edge predominated. I will now begin by looking at the design for a black dial clock which I find especially attractive, and in many ways more so than the equivalent white dial clock.

Black dial clock

This clock design is measured from a rare early black dial clock c.1760, which has a spring wound fusee compensated movement with a

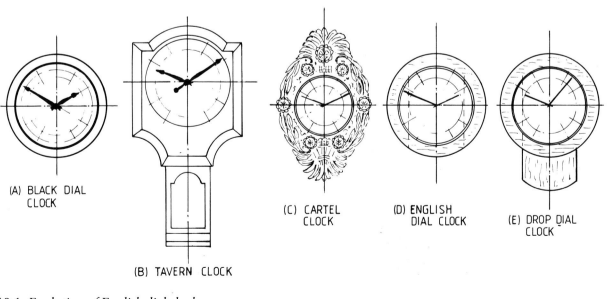

(A) BLACK DIAL CLOCK

(B) TAVERN CLOCK

(C) CARTEL CLOCK

(D) ENGLISH DIAL CLOCK

(E) DROP DIAL CLOCK

10.1 *Evolution of English dial clocks*

10.2 *Black dial clock*

10.3 *Casework of black dial clock*

'tic-tac' escapement embracing only 2½ teeth. The black painted dial is 425mm (16¾in) diameter and is signed 'Webster, London', and has gold coloured Roman and Arabic numerals and annular rings on the surround. The heart shaped hands are original and the minute hand is balanced.

The salt box case is made of oak and the dial board is of mahogany. The case back has typical salt box projections top and bottom, and a hinged door either side externally edged on three sides. The dial board, which is peg fixed to the salt box, is known to have been repainted black from white, but the wide concave profile of the edge surround, and the fact that the clock has no bezel or glass gives confidence to believe that its original colour was black. Another indicator that it is an early black dial clock is revealed by the casework which is a plain butt glued assembly. Later English dial clock cases used half joints and dovetail connections. The use of mahogany for the dial board however does suggest the case could not be much earlier than say 1760.

Construction

The general arrangement is shown in Fig 10.4 and sectional details in Figs 10.5 and 10.6. A rear view of the dial board is given in Fig 10.6 which includes miscellaneous details of the hands and pegs. It is an especially easy case to make because of its all wood construction, and the fact that there is no glass bezel or a metal dial plate to fit. The construction is in two parts comprising the dial board and the salt box.

Salt box

The salt box consists of items (2), (3) and (4). As mentioned above the original case has no joints, the items simply being cut to size, cleaned up and butt glued together. Cut the openings for the side doors prior to assembly while the case components are still loose. Make the hinged side doors to the dimensions shown on the general arrangement and in section 'BB'. The raised edged surround (6) of the side doors is typical of this early period, and they are held closed by small twist catches (10). A sanding drum is useful for cleaning up the concave sections of the salt box back.

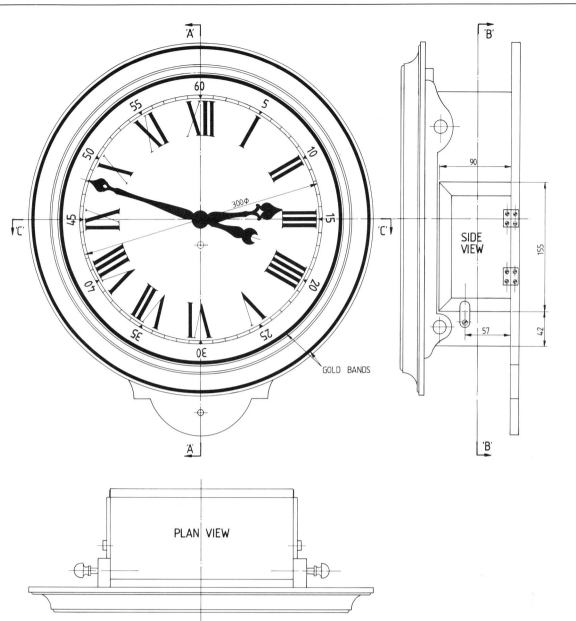

10.4 *General arrangement of black dial clock*

Dial board

The dial board is a one piece construction. As noted above the original material is mahogany, but since the finish on this item is painted all over, there is no reason why a utilitarian hardwood such as beech should not be used. The method of turning the dial board so that there are no unsightly screw holes on the back when completed is as follows. First, mount the dial board onto a plywood backing disc to act as a sandwich between this and the bowl turning head. Secure the two together from the back with screws in the positions where the registers (7), (8) will later be fixed. Then screw fix this

assembly from behind to the lathe faceplate. After machining and finishing split the items apart and add on the registers (7) and (8). These will cover the screw holes used for turning. The side registers (7) have peg holes for fixing the dial board to the case, and the top register (8) is an aid to aligning these with the holes on the case. Cramp the dial board and case together when drilling through the four 6mm diameter peg holes. Spindle turn the pegs (9) to details as in Fig 10.7. Recessed dial boards should always be rough machined first and set aside to allow for wood movement. If this is not done then even with the driest of timbers the back will bow to a convex profile.

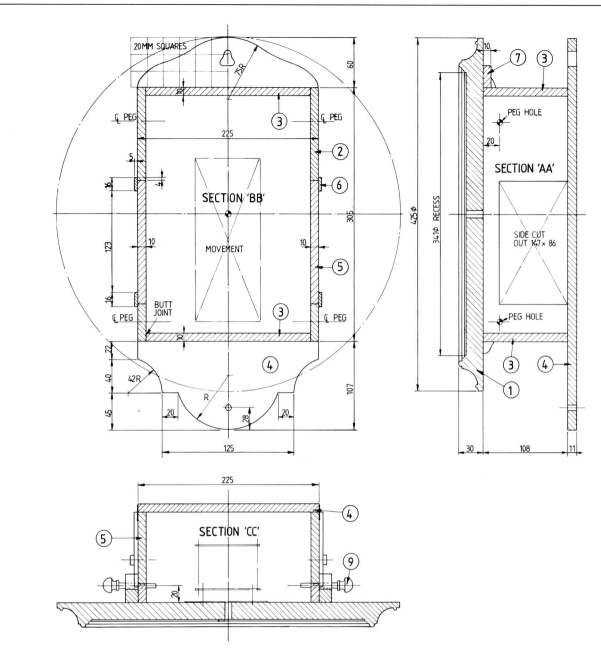

10.5 *Sectional arrangement of black dial clock*

Hands

There are two choices for the hands, you can either make them from steel plate and gold paint them, or alternatively you can cut them from brass plate. There are no commercial sources of ready made hands that I know of, but being fairly large they are not difficult to hand cut. Coat the brass plate with engineer's marking ink prior to setting out, so that the scribe marking is much easier to follow when saw cutting. When finished clean up and polish them and then fit them to the movement.

Finish

Paint the dial board a semi-gloss black on the front and a matt black finish on the back. Carefully set out the gold Roman and Arabic numerals prior to gilding these. The Roman numerals are 42mm high and the Arabic ones 13mm. As a guide the thickness of the broad stroke of Roman numerals is usually about 10 per cent of the numeral height (i.e. 3.5–4mm), but on finer dials this proportion tends to be less. The gold minute ring is 300mm O.D. and 4.5mm wide. A compass fitted with a pair of

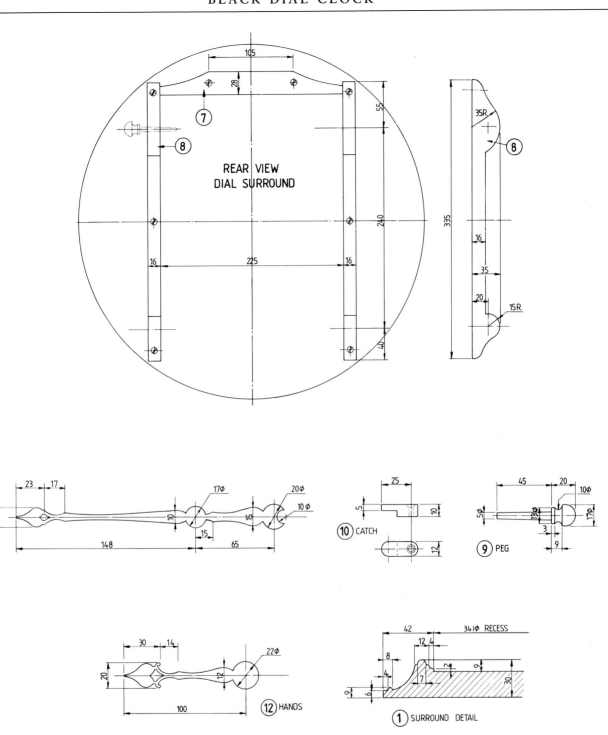

10.6 *Miscellaneous details of black dial clock*

spring bows will be needed to apply the gold size. Experiment on a piece of scrap board before proceeding to paint the dial. The salt box case should be stained a light or medium oak, and after sealing apply two rubbers of French polish followed by a good application of wax polish.

Movement

Fit an eight day spring wound movement with pendulum regulation. As explained in earlier chapters movements are commonly posted off the dial plate, but of course the black dial clock does not have one. Instead the movement is posted off a false plate screw fixed to the back of the dial board. Alternatively the movement could be fixed by brackets to the dial board.

PARTS LIST

Item	No	Material	Dimensions (mm)
1 Dial board	1	Mahogany	430sq×30 thick
2 Salt box side	2	Oak	108×10×305 long
3 Salt box top/bottom	2	Oak	108×10×205 long
4 Salt box back	1	Oak	225×11×472 long
5 Side door	2	Oak	86×10×147 long
6 Side door edge	2	Oak	16×5×350 long each
7 Top register	1	Mahogany	28×10×225 long
8 Side register	2	Mahogany	35×16×335 long
9 Peg	4	Oak	22sq×80 long
10 Door catch	2	Oak	12×10×32 long
11 Door hinge	4	Brass	10 wide×20 long
12 Hands	1 set	Brass plate	Cut to suit detail given
13 Movement	1	–	Eight day spring wound c/w pendulum

CHAPTER 11

Tavern clocks

In 1797 an Act of Parliament was passed whereby an annual tax was levied on clocks and watches owned by the public. The duty varied according to the type of clock or watch you had. On clocks it was five shillings, a gold watch cost ten shillings, and silver or metal watch two shillings and six pence. It was a difficult tax to enforce depending on the public to declare ownership, which they were naturally loathe to do. It was so unpopular that it temporarily decimated the clock and watch industry before the Act was repealed nine months later. Clocks which did not come under the act were those in coaching inns, taverns and public places, and as a consequence tavern clocks became more commonly known as 'Act of Parliament' clocks. However, the title is a misnomer for tavern clocks were made for some 80 years before the government legislation of 1797.

Styles

Tavern clocks are large wall mounted clocks with a dial typically 600–700mm (24–28in) wide, with a narrow case behind housing a weight driven movement, an anchor escapement and a seconds pendulum. The earliest, c.1720, had a simple square shield back with a broken arch top and a short case below as in Fig 11.1(A). Slightly later (by 1735) tavern clock dials had become rectangular (B), and by 1750 the shield had developed arched bottom corners as in (C). After this tavern clock styles became more changeable, with the appearance of the octagonal dial (D) and finally the circular white dial (E), the latter lasting until about 1840. In the years up to 1780 the cases were predominantly black painted with gold numerals, minute rings and hands, and the trunk casework was frequently decorated with chinoiserie scenes. Later ones had cases veneered with mahogany or walnut. Shield back clocks were typically made from three or four flat vertical boards surrounded by an edge moulding picture frame style, and octagonal and round dials usually had a horizontal board configuration. Many tavern clocks originate from the Home Counties and East Anglia, and bear the inscription of the maker's name and township. On shield dials this was at the base of the shield above the surround, and on round or octagonal tavern clocks on the trunk below the dial. The casework was mostly a simple straight sided box with a sloped back moulded base. Octagonal and round dial clocks also had additional ear pieces on the sides. In the 1790s a tear drop shaped case with a coopered construction also evolved. It is possible that the shape of this could have been influenced by the curved form of balloon clocks (see Chapter 6) also being made at this time, though this is largely conjecture. Trunk doors mostly reflect the shape of the dial board. Thus shield style tavern clocks have doors with a broken arch top mirroring the shield profile, and those on round dial clocks have a radiused concave top.

Although the case trunk appears to vary in length with different dial shapes the effect is largely visual due to the dial size. Their length is in fact fairly consistent, typically 1200–1400mm (48in–55in). The hands on early tavern clocks were of solid form and on later ones pierced. Because of their size minute hands were always balanced to minimize the power requirements and wear on the movement. With the exception of late tavern clocks, dials were always marked with both Roman and Arabic numerals.

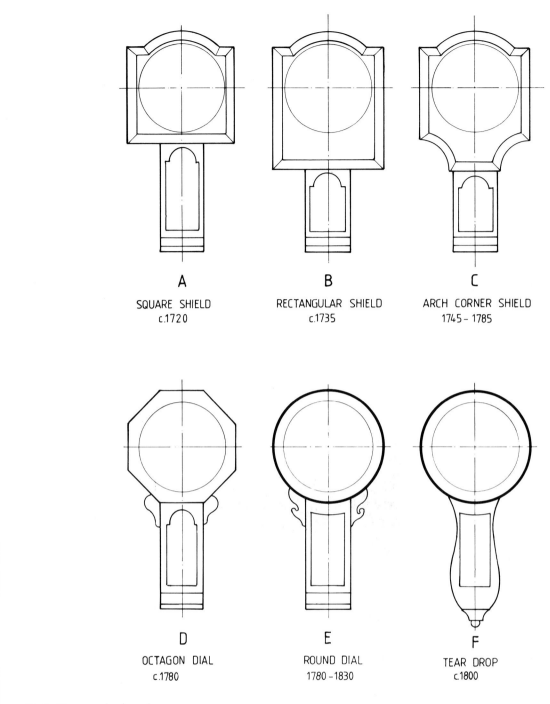

A
SQUARE SHIELD
c.1720

B
RECTANGULAR SHIELD
c.1735

C
ARCH CORNER SHIELD
1745 – 1785

D
OCTAGON DIAL
c.1780

E
ROUND DIAL
1780 – 1830

F
TEAR DROP
c.1800

11.1 *Tavern clock styles*

Tavern clock designs

Designs for four different styles of tavern clocks are given including two with round dials, one with a shield dial, and one with an octagonal dial. The principal design is measured from a round white dial tavern clock c. 1820 having Roman numerals only, and the others are derivatives of this. A feature common to them all is the size of the painted dial and the Roman numerals which are 500mm O.D. and 65mm high.

This numeral height is quite common on tavern clocks, though sometimes 75mm or even larger numerals are found. Like the black dial clock in the last chapter tavern clocks do not have glass bezels so from a casework aspect are easy to make.

11.2 *Round dial tavern clock*

11.3 *Tavern clock trunk*

Construction

The general arrangement for the smaller round dial tavern clock is shown in Fig 11.4 and sectional details in Fig 11.5. Miscellaneous sections and enlarged details are given in Fig 11.6. The construction is in two parts, the dial and the case.

Dial board

Begin construction by making the dial board which consists of three horizontal planks of wood (17) butt glued together. Then strengthen this with two side register strips (18) which also serve to locate the dial board to the case. Secure the dial board to the case by pegs (19) fitting through holes drilled in the register strips/case sides. The original clock had no top register but it is probably a good idea to fix one on as it makes it easier to locate the dial board in the correct position for pegging. The method of machining the dial board so there are no visible screw holes in the back is similar to that for the black dial clock (Chapter 10), and to turn one as large as this the lathe speed needs to be quite low, typically 200–300 rpm.

Casework

The case consists of the top (1), sides (2), cross rails (5), (6), side strips (4) and a back (3) which you should cut to the details as in sections 'AA', 'BB' and 'CC'. Dovetail joint the top and sides (see Fig 11.4), and half joint the cross rails (5) and (6) behind the side strips (4). Elsewhere the case is butt jointed. Assemble these items and glue them together with additional pinning if required. An alternative case form I have seen on tavern clocks is one where the back spans the full case width and is pinned/glued to the top and sides from the behind. This has the disadvantage that there is a visible joint to be seen on the outside.

Complete the casework by adding other items, including the base ogee moulding (9), base strips (10) and (11) and the earpieces (16). The ogee moulding is only a short length and is probably best worked by hand. The base surround (12), which has a bead/coving profile, is very similar to that used on the broken arch bracket clock featured in Chapter 4. Fretsaw the earpieces to

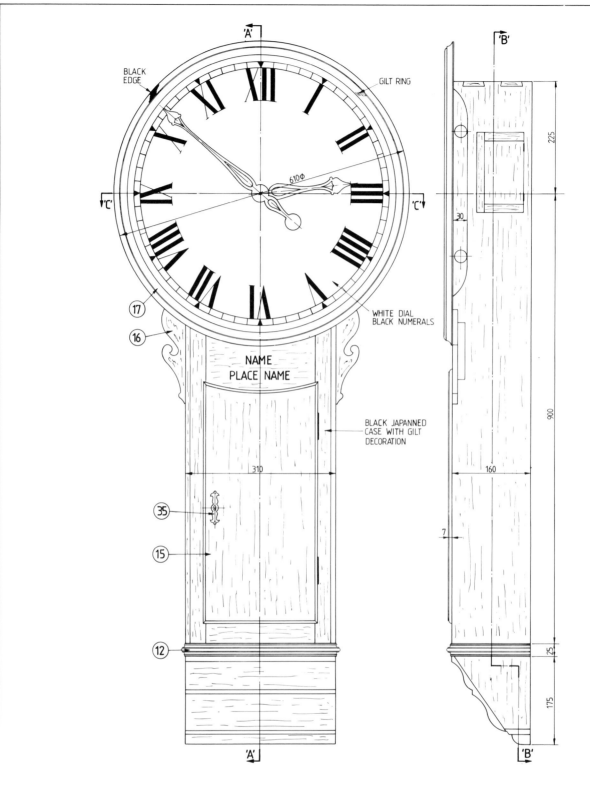

BLACK EDGE

GILT RING

610∅

WHITE DIAL
BLACK NUMERALS

⑰
⑯

NAME
PLACE NAME

BLACK JAPANNED
CASE WITH GILT
DECORATION

310

㉟

⑮

⑫

225

30

900

160

7

25

175

11.4 *General arrangement of round dial tavern clock*

the shape shown, clean them up and glue fix
these to the case with additional fillet behind.
Next construct the hinged side doors (13) which
are similar to those on the black dial clock with
external edging (14) on three sides. Fit a small

wooden twist catch to hold each door closed.
Their position seems to be variable. On the
original they were mounted rather high up at
65mm down from the top of the case, but I have
seen others where they are level with the seat

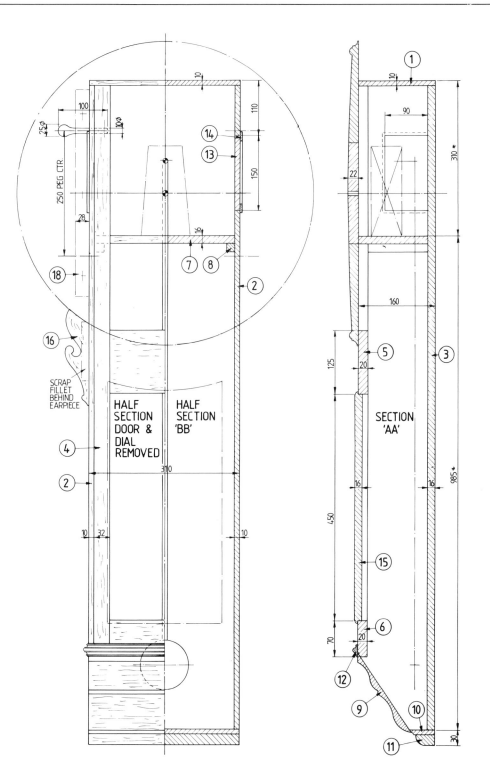

11.5 *Sectional arrangement of round dial tavern clock*

board. In this design I have therefore opted for a middle position. The trunk door is a single panel profiled at the top to match the dial curvature, and with a quarter round bead machined all round. Hinge the door to the case and fit a lock and escutcheon as shown.

Movement and hands

Tavern clocks were typically fitted with simple weight driven movements having a seconds pendulum for regulation. Most movements produced today which have seconds pendulums

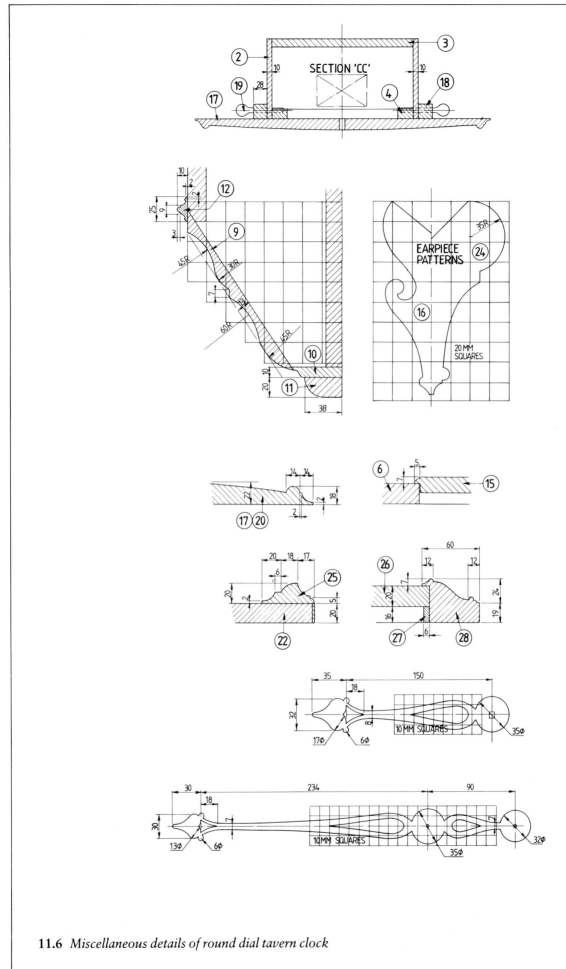

11.6 *Miscellaneous details of round dial tavern clock*

are made for longcase clocks and have striking and chiming arrangements, and these are too sophisticated and expensive for this application. There would be problems anyway in incorporating one of these, because the wheel ratios are designed to accommodate a weight drop of about 1.5m. What you really need is a simple weight driven timepiece suitable for a wall clock, but you may have to do a bit of searching among horological dealers to find one with a seconds pendulum. A possible compromise could be a weight driven movement suitable for a wall clock with a 590mm (22in) pendulum which is more readily available. These typically require a 900mm case height for the weights to drive an eight day movement, which the tavern clock case will accommodate. Occasionally a tavern clock was fitted with a passing strike so it would be acceptable to fit a movement which had this facility. Make sure the motion has sufficient power to drive the hands. The movement is not posted off the dial as for other clocks, but fixed independently to the seatboard. You then peg fix the dial board to the case, and add the cut and polished brass hands on afterwards. One further point to check is that there is enough projection of the centre wheel pin/cannon pin through the dial board to attach the hands to the motion work. Do not forget to drill a hole through the dial board for the winding key!

Finishing

The dial is white painted with black numerals, and is black edged with a gilt inner ring. The original black Japanned finish with gilt decoration on the casework is obviously going to be hard to match unless one is sufficiently skilled. I suggest that you apply a matt black or silk finish (not a high gloss). Tavern clocks do exist with plain black cases devoid of gilt decoration and you could leave it at that. Most people though, would, I am sure, like to add some form of decoration and I have following suggestions. You could make decorative stencil patterns and use a gold spray paint can to apply the design to the trunk and the earpieces. This is a technique I have seen applied quite successfully on painted furniture, but do experiment first on a piece of scrap wood. Another possibility, occasionally seen on tavern clocks, is to paste a suitable pastel coloured picture onto the trunk

and lacquer over this to seal it against dirt. You could also veneer the case in mahogany or walnut as were tavern clocks in the later years. A final personal touch you can add, just as the tavern clockmakers did, is to inscribe your name and the place where the clock was made on the trunk below the dial board.

Alternative tavern clock designs

Figs 11.7 and 11.8 give design details for three other tavern clocks. The left section on Fig 11.7 gives dimensions for a larger round dial tavern clock with the addition of Arabic numerals external to the minute ring, and that on the right shows a shield style tavern clock. Fig 11.8 gives dimensions for an octagonal style dial tavern clock. It should be noted that most earlier tavern clocks always had both Roman and Arabic

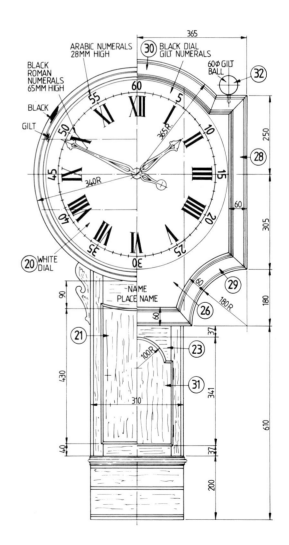

11.7 *Arrangement of large round dial/shield dial tavern clocks*

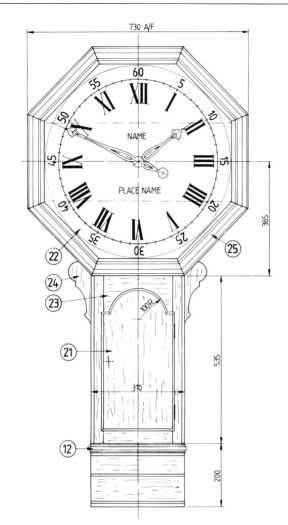

numerals, hence their inclusion on these case designs. The cases are broadly similar for all three alternatives apart from variations in the position and size of the cross rails, and the style of the trunk doors and ear pieces. You should make the round and octagonal dial boards from three horizontal planks, and the shield dial tavern clock from vertical boards. With regard to finish, paint the shield dial clock black with gilt numerals and add casework decoration as for the small round dial clock described earlier. The round and octagonal dial tavern clocks, however, could be veneered with woods such as mahogany and walnut as mentioned above.

Finally, if the reader is interested in seeing examples of early tavern clocks there are three in Snowshill Manor (N.T.). Two of these are shield dials and the other is a round dial, though unfortunately without its case. Interestingly one of the shield dials has an error in that both the nine o'clock and eleven o'clock numerals are shown as 'XI'. One of the clocks has an extra feature of an additional small door on the sloped backed base section. This is useful for setting the pendulum bob regulating nut which tends to be below the level of the trunk bottom door and difficult to get at.

11.8 *Arrangement of octagonal dial tavern clock*

PARTS LIST

Item	No	Material	Dimensions (mm)
Round dial case (1)			
1 Top	1	Pine	160×10×310 long
2 Side	2	Pine	160×10×1295 long
3 Back	1	Pine	140×16×1295 long
4 Side strip	2	Pine	32×20×1140 long
5 Cross rail (1)	1	Pine	125×20×290 long
6 Cross rail (2)	1	Pine	70×20×290 long
7 Seat board	1	Pine	144×16×290 long
8 Support strip	2	Pine	16sq×130 long
9 Ogee moulding (1)	1	Pine	200×13×310 long
10 Base strip	1	Pine	52×10×310 long
11 Base capping strip	1	Pine	38×20×310 long
12 Case moulding strip	1	Pine	32×10×700 long
13 Side door	2	Pine	90×10×150 long
14 Side door edge strip	1	Pine	16×4×750 long
15 Trunk door	1	Pine	236×16×500 long

16	Earpiece (1)	2	Pine	60×10×200 long
17	Round dial board	1	Pine	210×30×1800 long. Split into three horizontal boards
18	Dial register strip	2	Pine	30×28×420 long
19	Peg	2	Pine	32sq×100 long

Round dial case (2)

| 20 | Round dial board (2) | 1 | Pine | 240×30×2000 long. Split into three horizontal boards |
| 21 | Trunk door (2) | 1 | Pine | 236×16×460 long |

Octagonal dial case

22	Octagonal dial board	1	Pine	250×20×2100 long. Split into three horizontal boards
23	Cross rail (3)	1	Pine	160×20×310 long
24	Earpiece (2)	2	Pine	75×10×200 long
25	Dial board edge moulding (1)	1	Pine	60×20×2600 long

Shield dial case

26	Shield dial board	1	Pine	160×20×3000 long. Split into four vertical boards
27	Backing strip	1	Pine	19×6×1500 long
28	Shield moulding (1)	1	Pine	60×43×2000 thick
29	Shield moulding (2)	1	Pine	200×43×600 long
30	Shield moulding (3)	2	Pine	140×43×280 long
31	Trunk door (3)	1	Pine	236×16×360 long
32	Ball finial	2	Pine	60 dia with gilt finish. Fix with dowel peg

Metalwork

33	Trunk door hinge	2	Brass	50 long×16 wide
34	Side door hinge	4	Brass	20 long×10 wide
35	Escutcheon plate	1	Brass	65×20 nominal size. Purchase to suit
36	Hands	1 pair	Brass	60×40×20 S.W.G. Cut to detail as shown
37	Movement	1	–	Eight day spring wound c/w seconds pendulum

CHAPTER 12

English dial clock
(c.1860)

One of the more enduring forms of English dial clock was the mid-nineteenth century design with rounded bottom casework. In Chapter 10 I briefly discussed the evolution of this clock but there is, in fact, rather more to it. In the 1770s the popularity of wall clocks with black dials declined in favour of white dials then being used more generally on all types of clock. The English salt box clock with a white dial introduced about this time, having casework similar to the black dial but with a narrow concave surround, was made up to about 1820. This design eventually gave way to one with a rounded bottom case which was to last for sixty or more years. In the new form the dial surround was convex instead of concave and was wider than that on the salt box clock. The plain square salt box lost its back projections top and bottom and the base became rounded to accommodate the longer pendulums then being used. The back was rebated into the sides which now extended the full case thickness. The earlier wooden dials, either inset or made as part of the surround were replaced by iron dials. The dial glass was typically convex, and by 1860 was fitted in spun brass bezels secured with plaster from behind. Dial clocks with flat glass bezels were still produced, however.

About 1800 the verge escapement was displaced in favour of the anchor escapement which resulted in other changes to the casework. The pendulum on a verge was usually carried directly off the end of the pallet arbor regulating the crown wheel, but on the anchor it is supported on an independent back cock slightly higher than the escape wheel and is driven by the escapement through a crutch. As a consequence the case side door that gave access to the pendulum was raised slightly. At the same time

the external edging strips were omitted to make the side door flush fitting. The bottom door was treated similarly but had cockbeading applied round the edge.

Another common case form produced in the mid-nineteenth century was the 'drum case', where instead of being straight sided as described above, the box was circular following the outline of the dial surround. This had a coopered construction.

While clocks with round dial surrounds were produced in large numbers, octagonal dial boards were also popular between 1830–1880. Drum style cases, however, are not suited to octagonal dials for obvious reasons. Fig 12.1 illustrates the predominant nineteenth century patterns.

Clock description

This clock design is based on an original English dial clock c. 1860. It is fitted with an eight day spring wound fusee movement with an anchor escapement, and has a nominal dial size 280mm (11in) O.D. It has a white dial plate with moon style hands, and a spun brass bezel fitted with convex glass secured with plaster. The dial is signed 'Christopher Snell, Selsby' in a typical mid-century position, the name being above the centre and the township below the winding square.

The mahogany case has typical period features, a rounded base section, a rebated back, and access doors in the side and base. The side door for access to the pendulum/movement is positioned slightly above the middle, and the bottom door for adjusting the pendulum rating nut has cockbeaded edges.

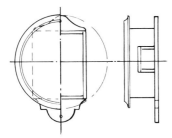

(A) SALT BOX

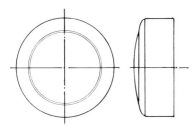

(B) DRUM CASE

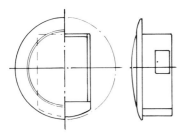

(C) ENGLISH DIAL

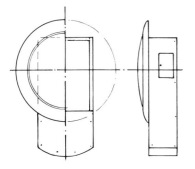

(D) DROP DIAL

12.1 *Typical nineteenth century English dial clock*

12.2 *English dial clock*

Construction

The general arrangement is given in Fig 12.3, sectional details in Fig 12.4, and dial surround details in Fig 12.5. As mentioned above, the original dial is 280mm (11in) O.D. This is a relatively uncommon size today and manufacturers have tended to standardize on 203mm (8in), 254mm (10in) and 305mm (12in) dials. The opportunity has therefore been taken to adjust the design upwards to 305mm (12in), selected mainly on the basis that it needed the minimum of change to the casework. For the historian the original dial surround was 400mm O.D. and the box width 240mm. If the dial plate size or the bezel fitting differs from the drawing then appropriate dimensional changes will need to be made to the dial surround, the casework bottom radius and possibly also the case width.

Casework

Commence construction by making the sides (2), top (3), bottom (4) and front panel (6). Cut these to the sizes given and rebate them together as shown. The curved base is of coopered construction, which you make by fitting narrow wood strips into small location rebates in the

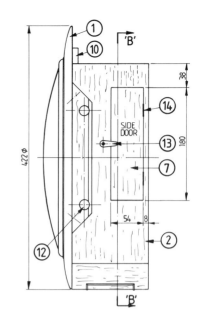

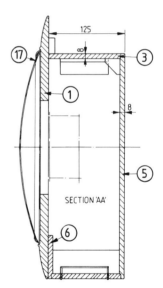

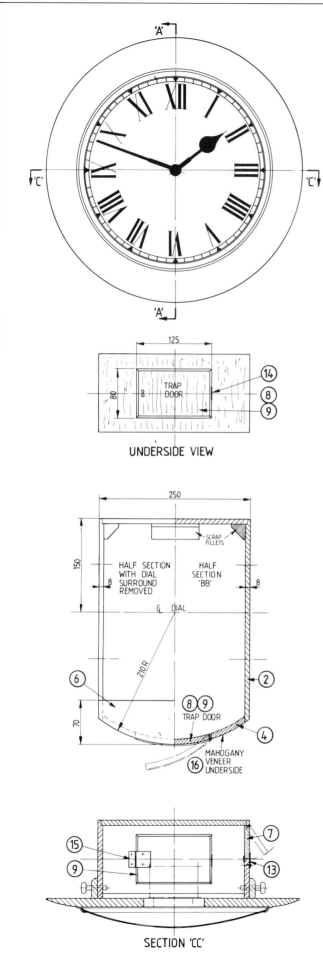

12.3 *General arrangement of English dial clock*

12.4 *Sectional arrangement of English dial clock*

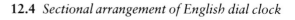

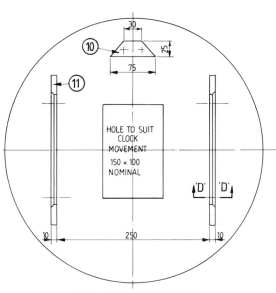

REAR VIEW-BOX REMOVED

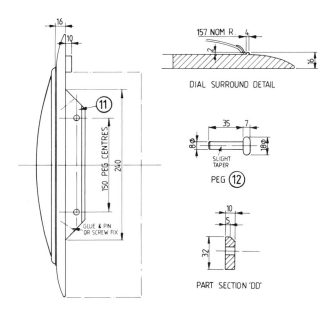

12.5 (Top & Above) *Dial surround details*

front and back panels. After gluing the assembly and cleaning up, veneer the case bottom with mahogany to conceal the jointing. In the original this is laid in the same direction as the coopering strips. Although there are disadvantages of doing it this way as opposed to laying it transverse (see page 45), seasoned mahogany is fairly stable so it probably will not matter whichever way you choose. Finish the casework by adding the hinged side and bottom door items (7) and (8), and fit cockbeading (9) round the latter.

Dial surround

The original dial surround (1) is a one piece construction with the wood grain horizontally aligned. Follow the woodturning procedure as described for the black dial clock (page 75). You should turn the front profile so that the brass bezel ring is a snug fit within the raised annular bead (see enlarged section Fig 12.5). Then complete the dial surround by adding the top and side registers (10) and (11), and fix this to the casework by the spindle turned pegs.

Movement, bezel and hands

First fix the dial plate on the surround. This is typically held in place by four to six small pins or screws fitting through holes in the perimeter, but the arrangement may vary depending on the dial plate you fit. Next fit the movement (eight day), either posted off the back of the dial plate or alternatively bracket fixed to the dial surround. Lastly fit the bezel ring (and sight ring if fitted), which again is usually held either by screws or pins onto the front of the surround in the recess provided.

The screw holes on the dial plate edge are concealed behind the bezel ring when this is closed. On the drawing the 'moon style' hands fitted on the original have been changed to spade pattern which are more readily available. These were used on English dial clocks for a large part of the nineteenth century. Dials with convex glass bezels were usually fixed with plaster behind the bezel ring. Bezels to suit flat glass are commonly two part assemblies and in case you should decide to fit one of these, some details of the arrangement are given as follows.

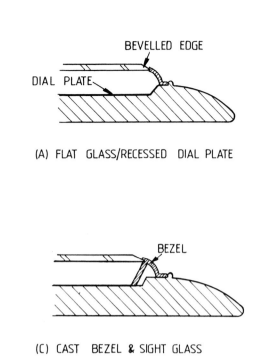

(A) FLAT GLASS/RECESSED DIAL PLATE

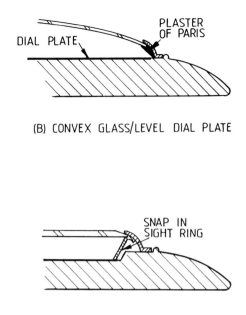

(B) CONVEX GLASS/LEVEL DIAL PLATE

(C) CAST BEZEL & SIGHT GLASS

(D) SEPARATE BEZEL & SIGHT RING

12.6 *Bezel rings and sight glasses*

Bezels, dials plates and sight glasses

Bezel glass fitted to English dial clocks is of two types, either convex or flat, and the fitting depends principally on the space needed for the hands. Typically 10–15mm space is required at the centre between the dial plate and the inside face of the glass and Fig 12.6 shows the two situations. If a flat glass bezel is being used then it is usually necessary to recess the dial surround to fit the dial plate to give sufficient clearance for the hands as in (A), e.g. black forest wall clock Chapter 13. Flat glass is bevelled on the edge for it to fit correctly in the bezel ring. If a convex bezel is used as in (B) this usually provides adequate clearance without the need to recess the dial board or at least only very little. To a degree it depends on the thickness of the bezel ring itself, for example the mid-century English dial clocks fitted with convex glass only need shallow bezel rings.

Some dials are fitted with what is known as a 'sight ring'. These are silvered rings fitted on inside of the opening section of the bezel ring and surround the minute ring when the bezel is closed, thus concealing the dial plate screw fixing behind. A sight ring can be cast as part of the bezel ring itself as in (C), or it can be a separate independent ring fixed inside the bezel as in (D) which also holds the glass in place. Where the sight ring is part of the casting the bezel glass is snapped into a finely machined recess from the front. This is a skilled operation which requires the glass to be carefully ground on the edges to achieve the correct fit. Where the sight ring is a loose item this usually snaps into the bezel ring behind and holds the glass in place. A bezel/sight ring purchased today is most likely to be a two part assembly. A small fabricated metal catch is fixed behind the dial surround to hold the bezel closed.

Alternative designs

If perhaps this clock size is too large for your requirements and you would prefer a smaller one, suited say to a 200mm or 250mm dial plate, there is no reason why the casework should not be scaled down appropriately after first checking the proposed movement and pendulum will fit correctly within the case. English dial clocks were made with oak casework besides mahogany, so this is an acceptable alternative choice.

PARTS LIST

Casework

Item	No	Material	Dimensions (mm)
1 Dial surround	1	Mahogany	430sq×20 thick
2 Case side	2	Mahogany	125×8×330 long
3 Case top	1	Mahogany	125×8×250 long
4 Case bottom	1	Mahogany	70×117×500 long total. Cut into strips to suit
5 Front panel	1	Mahogany	70×8×250 long
6 Side door	1	Mahogany	54×8×180 long
7 Cockbeading	1	Mahogany	20×3×420 long
8 Top register	1	Mahogany	30×10×75 long
9 Side register	2	Mahogany	32×10×240 long
10 Peg	4	Mahogany	22sq×65 long
11 Catch	1	Mahogany	10×2×30 long

Miscellaneous

Item	No	Material	Dimensions (mm)
12 Hinge	3	Brass	Purchase to suit
13 Lock	1	Brass	Purchase to suit
14 Veneer	1	Mahogany	300×140 piece to cover bottom
15 Bezel & glass	1	Brass/ picture glass	305mm nominal diameter c/w bezel glass
16 Dial plate	1	White gloss metal	305mm nominal size
17 Hands	1 set	Blued steel	Moon style or alternatively spade pattern
18 Movement	1	–	Eight day spring wound c/w pendulum

CHAPTER 13

Black Forest wall clock

(c.1880)

Now here is an interesting timepiece which at first sight might appear to be just another English dial clock (Fig 13.1). Closer inspection, however, soon reveals it is not English and it is in fact a German Black Forest wall clock c.1890. Externally the initial giveaway is the rather basic skewer pin fixing of the dial surround to the casework and also that there is no name on the dial. Then when you look inside the case and find a simple wooden frame movement with just a few brass wheels you are left in no doubt and realize just how basic the design is. Yet despite their simplicity and cheapness these German clocks are nonetheless attractive, durable and collectable pieces.

History

The Black Forest area of Germany has been the centre of a clock making industry for at least two hundred years, a tradition which it still maintains today. In the nineteenth century a large part of the production was exported to England, and in the second half of the century this became fiercely competitive with the Americans joining in the fray. As a result there was a trend for ever increasing simplicity and cheapness. In the very earliest Black Forest clock movements the wheels as well as the framework were made from wood. Later, when brass wheels and steel arbors were introduced, these were fitted in rolled brass ferrules in the wooden front and back plates. The wheel work was very simple and the anchor escapement typically had pallets formed out of a bent steel strip. Eventually, by the turn of the century, the movements also had brass framework in the face of stiff competition from America.

13.1 *Black Forest dial clock*

There was a strong emphasis on simple fixtures. In Figs 13.3 and 13.7 you can see the cheap skewer pins fixture used on the dial surround have been used to fix the back plate of the movement, and then the movement to the seatboard. Nails rather than screws were extensively used: for example, on the clock here, the hinges on the side and bottom doors are nailed on, as are the dial surround register strips. The door catches are very basic, the bottom one consisting of a leaf shaped knob with a small steel screw through it and a catchplate behind. The latter is fitted over a thread section filed square, with sufficient thread remaining on the corners for a nut to be screwed on to fix the plate down. The side door catch was even simpler, consisting of a round brass knob with a bent nail through it, though I did wonder if this was a replacement. I doubt if you could get more basic than this. Finally, on the casework itself, I found that the Black Forest clock makers had economized even further by making the back panel of two pieces of wood butt glued together.

Clock description

The clock has an octagonal dial surround fitted with a white dial plate nominally 225mm (9in) O.D., a flat glass bezel, and has moon style hands. There was no name on the dial plate which had suffered some yellowing and crazing due to age. The dial surround and casework is walnut veneered over a pine base structure, and features brass inlay work a revival from the Regency period. A side door provides access to the movement and a bottom door for adjusting the pendulum rating nut. The drop box has a glazed lenticule opening for the pendulum and carved earpieces on each side. The wooden frame movement is fitted with brass wheel work and steel arbors and pinions, and has a pendulum with approximately a half seconds beat.

13.2 *Earpiece detail on Black Forest dial clock*

13.3 *Wooden plated movement*

Construction

The general arrangement is shown in Fig 13.4, casework sections in Fig 13.5 and miscellaneous details in Fig 13.6. A drawing of the movement framework is also given in Fig 13.7. The drawings are based on a nominal dial size of 225mm (9in). If a different dial size is fitted proportional adjustments to the casework will need to be made. The construction is in two parts, i.e. the dial surround and the casework.

Dial surround

Begin construction of the dial surround (1) by preparing a length of straight board chamfered on one side and then divide it up into segment pieces. Fig 13.6 shows the dial board and the rectangular cut out in the middle. Cutting and

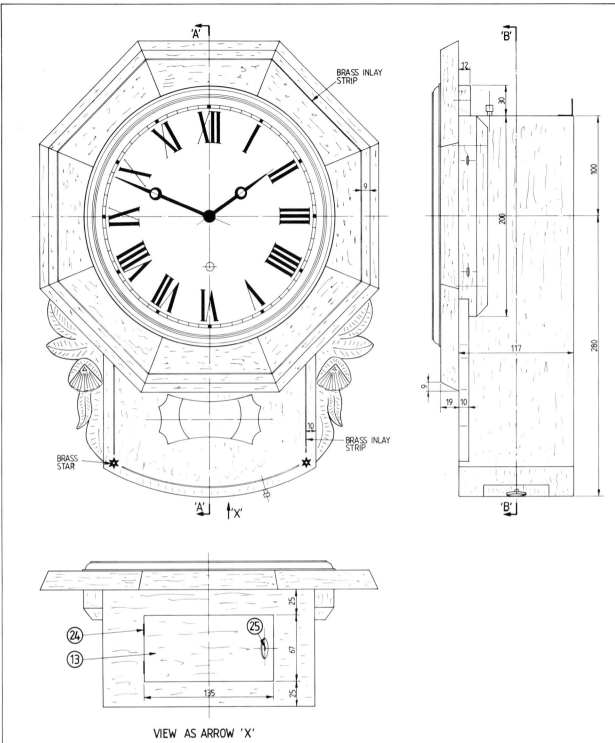

13.4 *General arrangement of Black Forest wall clock*

fitting segments by hand is never easy but with a little patience and care you should be able to achieve a respectable result. Circular saw benches and radial arm saws if available do make it easier to cut the 22½ degree angles accurately. After gluing and setting the segment pieces, woodturn a recess in the dial surround

ready to receive the dial plate. This is needed to provide sufficient clearance for the hands assuming that flat bezel glass is being fitted (see Fig 12.6). Finally add the top and side registers (11) and (12). Note that the left side register (looking on the clock face) has a cut out for the bezel catch.

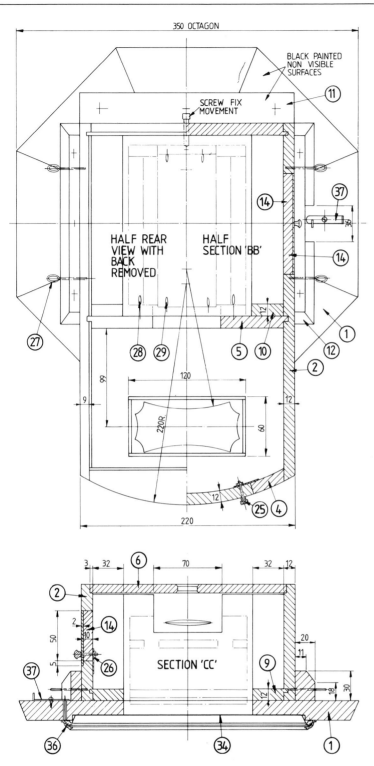

13.5 *Sectional arrangement of Black Forest wall clock*

Casework

The casework jointing is a tongue grooved/rebated construction broadly similar to dial clocks in previous chapter though there are notable differences. The back board, for example, is a removable item to gain access to the movement. This is required because the movement is pinned to a seatboard and is not posted off the dial plate as on English dial clocks. To remove the dial surround, you first open the bezel and remove the hands, and then unpin the side registers (12). The thumb hole in the back board is to enable you to lift the latter

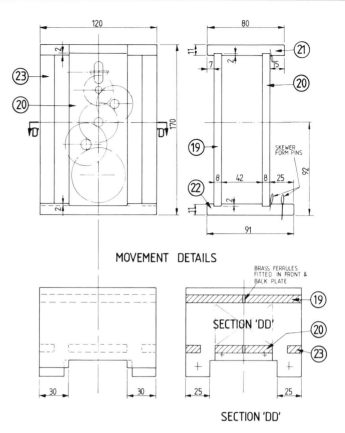

MOVEMENT DETAILS

SECTION 'DD'

SECTION 'DD'

13.7 Details of wooden plated movement

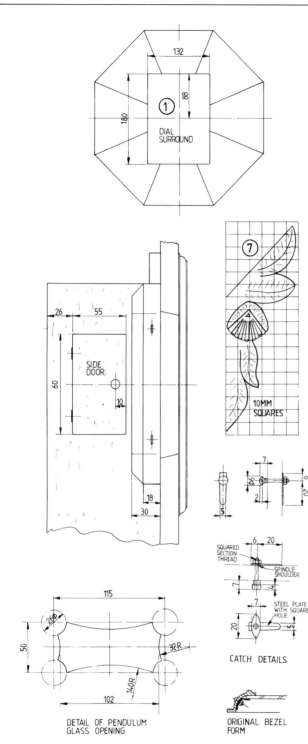

13.6 Miscellaneous details of Black Forest wall clock

out from the case not to support the clock. The wall plate for hanging the clock is a separate fixture.

Make the case by first preparing the top (3), sides (2), and seatboard (5), and tongue joint these together as indicated. If you are uncertain of the final position of the seatboard, consider mounting this on side strips rather than fitting it

into grooves as shown on the drawing. The drop dial board (8) and the front strips (9) were assumed to be tongue jointed to the sides, but this was difficult to verify without dismantling the clock completely. It is assumed that item (9) is glued on strip work, and I suggest that you make it this way. Assemble items (2), (3), (5), (8), (9) and (15), and fit and glue them together as a group. Make sure you complete the opening for the glass lenticule in the drop dial panel prior to assembly. Note that the rebate in the sides to fit the back board (6) is carried through to the base, and the bottom rail (15) is lap jointed accordingly to fit into this. Form the door opening at the bottom of the drop box by insetting strips into rebates in the inside edges of items (8) and (15) (see section 'AA'). Lay two strips along the sides of the door, and the end pieces front to back. Make the side and bottom door to the details shown in Figs 13.5 and 13.6 and hinge them to suit. Also make the door catches and fit them as shown. Fit a catchplate style knob to the side door rather than a bent nail as in the original.

Movement and dial

In Fig 13.7 I have given details of the wooden movement framework more from an historical aspect rather than a constructional one. While it is not impossible to build it given the necessary horological and metalwork skills it is assumed that a conventional eight day spring wound movement will be fitted either posted off the dial plate or bracket fixed to the dial surround. With a posted arrangement it is of course possible to remove the dial surround from the casework without undoing the hands. Screw or pin fix the dial plate to the surround through small holes in the perimeter, and then fix the flat glass bezel in front. Finally fit the lenticule glass for the pendulum opening in the drop box.

Veneering and finishing

Finish by veneering the clock externally with walnut and apply brass inlay to details as shown on the drawings. Paint the back of the dial surround a matt black and polish the casework externally.

PARTS LIST

Item	No	Material	Dimensions (mm)
Casework			
1 Dial surround	1	Pine	115×19×1000 long
2 Case side	2	Pine	117×12×360 long
3 Case top	1	Pine	117×12×220 long
4 Case bottom	1	Pine	99×20×115 long
5 Seat board	1	Pine	95×12×206 long
6 Back panel	1	Pine	202×9×350 long
7 Carved side panel	2	Walnut	60×10×270 long total for both
8 Drop dial panel	1	Pine	195×12×206 long
9 Front strip	2	Pine	32×12×180 long
10 Side strip	2	Pine	32×12×95 long
11 Top register	1	Pine	30×12×220 long
12 Side register	2	Pine	30×20×200 long
13 Bottom door	1	Pine	67×22×135 long
14 Side door	1	Pine	50×10×100 long. 2 thick walnut veneer piece
15 Bottom rail	1	Pine	37×16×220 long
16 Beading	1	Pine	6×3×360 long
17 Veneer	–	Walnut	Veneer externally over all visible external surfaces
18 Glass	1	Picture glass	120×60
Movement framework (optional)			
19 Front plate	1	Pine	120×8×152 long
20 Back plate	1	Pine	60×8×152 long
21 Top board	1	Pine	80×11×120 long
22 Base board	1	Pine	91×11×120 long
23 Support post	2	Pine	15×8×152 long
Metalwork components			
24 Hinge	4	Brass	10 wide × 13 long. For trap/side doors
25 Trap door catch	1	Brass/steel	Make to details shown
26 Side door catch	1	Brass/steel	Make to details shown
27 Fixing pin (1)	4	Steel	3 dia, bend to suit. To fix items 1 & 12
28 Fixing pin (2)	2	Steel	2 dia, bend to suit. To fix item 22

29	Fixing pin (3)	4	Steel	1.5 dia, bend to suit. To fix item 20
30	Set screw	1	Steel	6mm isometric. To fix movement down
31	Inlay fretwork	–	Brass	1 thick brass fretwork & star emblems cut to suit
32	Wall bracket	1	Steel	Purchase to suit

Movement & dial

33	Movement	1	–	See notes
34	Dial	1	Steel plate	225 nominal dia, white dial
35	Hands	1 set	Blued steel	Moon style
36	Bezel/glass	1	Brass	Hinged bezel to suit dial. Nominal 225 dia c/w flat glass. Purchase to suit
37	Bezel catch	1	Brass	Fabricate to suit

CHAPTER 14

Cuckoo clock

One of the more unusual branches of horology is the study of cuckoo clocks. These are quite different from conventional bracket and wall clocks and instead of striking the hour on a bell, do so using a pair of wooden pipes which mimic the 'cuckoo call', while at the same time a miniature cuckoo bird emerges from a door on the casework. They were first made over two hundred years ago by the Black Forest clock makers, initially as a cottage industry and subsequently mass produced. Besides making cuckoo striking clocks the German horologists improvized further to produce others with quails, trumpets, flutes, gongs and musical chimes. A prominent feature on the casework was the carving of vines, leaves, birds and animal scenes, the inspiration drawn from life in the Black Forest and skilfully executed. The earliest cuckoo clocks date from around 1750, and by 1800 there was a thriving industry producing them. The two most famous cuckoo

clock makers were Theodor Ketterer (1815–1884) and Johann Baptist Beha (1815–1898), and between them and others an incredible range of cuckoo clocks were produced in an industry which survives today.

Styles

Fig 14.1 shows the most common cuckoo clock styles. The first two (A) and (B) are early shield clocks with a painted paper face c.1760. The roof top cuckoo clock (C) sometimes referred to as 'railroad-gate attendant' style is typically 1860–1870, and the carved cuckoo clock (D) decorated with vines, leaves, birds and animals also of similar date. The vast majority were wall mounted weight driven clocks, and the weights were commonly of a 'forest cone' pattern. While the dates quoted are for period cases all these styles tended to be produced one way or another

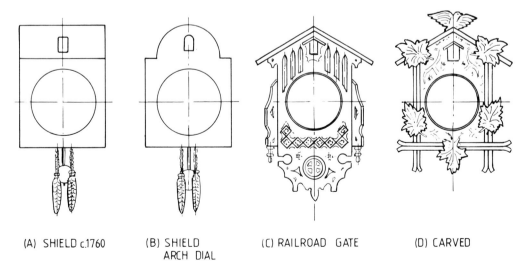

(A) SHIELD c.1760   (B) SHIELD ARCH DIAL   (C) RAILROAD GATE   (D) CARVED

14.1 *Cuckoo clock case styles*

101

through into the twentieth century while constructional aspects changed accordingly as time progressed. Early nineteenth century movements had wooden frames with brass wheelwork and steel pinions and arbors, but by 1900 the framework then had brass plates.

Cuckoo clock collection

In the search for a suitable cuckoo clock design I was fortunate to find the Tabley Old School Cuckoo Clock Collection. This museum has about three hundred clocks and easily surpasses equivalent Black Forest collections. The range extends from the smallest at about 100mm high to a large wall clock with a seconds pendulum, and there is even one with a carved life size cuckoo. All the styles mentioned above can be seen, and some have the most incredible carved forest scenes. Besides cuckoos there are quails and trumpeters, and also 'picture frame' cuckoo clocks with portraits of people and animals with eyes which roll in unison with the pendulum.

Clock design

From the collection I chose an attractive gothic style cuckoo clock which I felt would be less demanding than one with vine and leaf carving. The clock is shown in Fig 14.2 and the movement in Figs 14.3 and 14.4. Additional details of the carving are given in Figs 14.5 and 14.6. The case is of the railroad gate attendant pattern with gothic carving on the front and buttressed corner pieces. There are two side doors, a bottom door for adjusting the pendulum rating nut, and a removable back for general access to the movement. The dial is nominally 180mm with Roman gothic style numerals and carved bone hands, and the movement is wooden framed with brass and steel wheelwork. The spring barrel is fusee compensated and the strike regulated by count wheel.

Striking mechanism

Before detailing the clock casework the cuckoo strike mechanism is briefly explained. There are two aspects, the emitting of the call and the

14.2 *Railroad attendant cuckoo clock*

14.3 *Cuckoo clock movement rear view*

triggered by a pin wheel, the latter being part of the count wheel strike train. The subsequent release of the push wires from each pin on the side of the pin wheel allows the weighted bellows to fall back, and the wind passing out of the pipes makes the 'cuckoo' call. The notched count wheel is seen at the back of the movement in Fig 14.3 and governs the number of calls the cuckoo pipes make at each hour.

The second part of the motion is the movement of the bird. The cuckoo is mounted on a 'bird post' consisting of an angled wire rod mounted in bearings off the movement and free to twist about a vertical axis. This can be seen in the corner of the movement in Fig 14.4. On the hour the 'bird post' is triggered to twist and the cuckoo swings forward into the door aperture, the latter opening by two small wires attached to the front of the cuckoo. The cuckoo itself is also given a tweek from behind by a further wire attached to the top of one of the bellows and the bird opens its beak and flaps its wings. After completion of the cuckoo calls the bird post is released and spring action retracts the bird into the casework, closing the doors in front of it.

14.4 *Cuckoo clock movement corner view*

mechanics of the cuckoo bird movement. The 'cuckoo call' uses two wooden wind pipes similar to an organ pipe but inverted. Closed pipes are used which are shorter than open ones to enable them to fit within the case. These are tuned to the notes A and F below middle C and are about 140mm and 175mm long. At the top of each wind pipe is a bellows made of goat kid. In action the bellows are lifted by push wires

14.5 *Gothic arch carving*

14.6 *Pendant and quatrefoil carving*

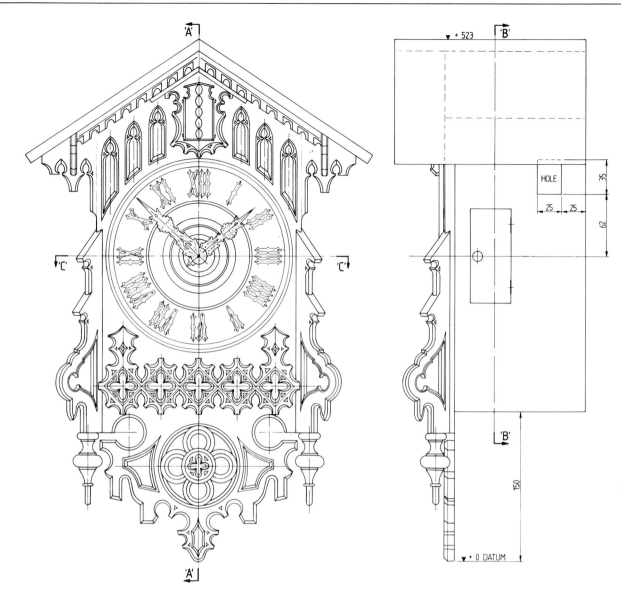

14.7 *General arrangement of cuckoo clock*

While the hour striking cuckoo clock is predominant, as mentioned earlier there are other striking arrangements such as quails, trumpeters, spiral gongs and musical boxes. A quail call is used to strike the quarter hours. The wind pipe for this is shorter than for cuckoo pipes, and the call is somewhat difficult to imitate correctly. In the trumpeter clock a trumpeter instead of a cuckoo moves out of the case on the hour, sounds a fanfare and then retreats. The trumpet sound is achieved by an adapted windbox arrangement with a series of metal cones tuned to the required notes.

Construction

The general arrangement is given in Fig 14.7 and sectional information in Fig 14.8. Enlarged details of the carving are shown in Fig 14.9. The construction is commenced with the box work and items progressively added. The movement, which is somewhat specialized, is discussed later in the chapter. As this might affect the casework details do study this before beginning construction.

With regard to materials cuckoo clock cases are traditionally made from woods such as

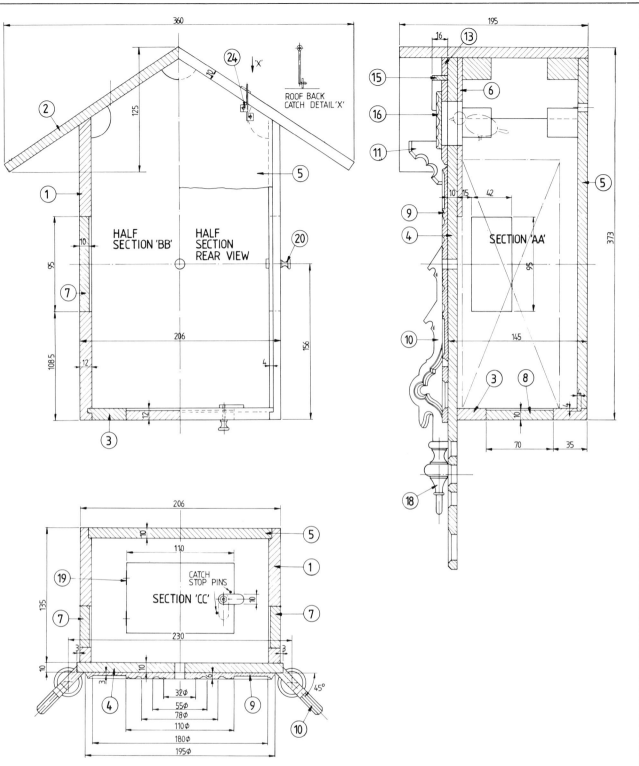

14.8 *Sectional arrangement of cuckoo clock*

'Linden' and spruce. 'Linden', or lime as it is more commonly known, is a carver's wood relatively knot free and easy to cut. It is thus ideally suited for the casework and especially the carved sections. Less frequently other woods such as oak, ash and walnut were used for the casework. If the back had a gong on it this would ideally be spruce chosen for its musical resonance, and for the framework of the movement more durable beech was used.

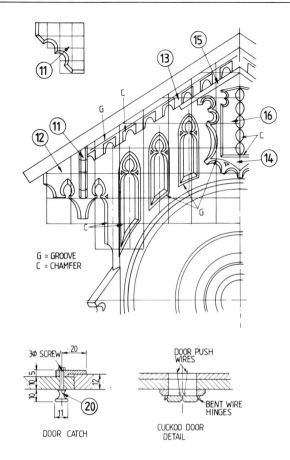

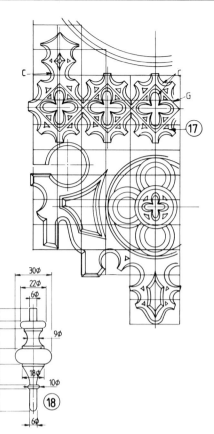

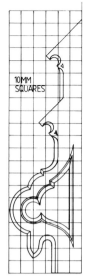

G = GROOVE
C = CHAMFER

3∅ SCREW

DOOR CATCH

DOOR PUSH WIRES

BENT WIRE HINGES

CUCKOO DOOR DETAIL

14.9 *Carving details*

Casework

Begin construction by making the casework including the sides (1), roof (2), bottom (3) and the frontpiece (4). Join the sides and bottom together using a tongue and groove connection, and also rebate the sides to fit the back (5). In addition groove item (3) to fit the lip at the bottom of the back. Then lay these items to one side while you make the front panel (4). The gothic design is shown on a grid pattern to help you transfer the pattern to the wood. If you are not an experienced carver experiment first on a piece of scrap lime wood to gain confidence. After completing the carving assemble the casework items (1) to (4) and check the fit. When this is satisfactory glue the case together, and strengthen the butt connections at the roof apex and the sides with wood fillet. After cleaning up then make and fit the back panel (5). This is a loose item, but is held firmly in place at the bottom by the lip connection just mentioned, and at the top by two metal brackets held closed by twist hooks screwed to the roof top (detail 'X'). Instead of fitting a wall bracket drill a hole in the back panel to hang the clock on the wall.

Carving

Besides the front panel a number of other items require carving and adding to the casework. These include the front and side gable end pieces (11) and (12), the gable edging (13) beneath the front roof, the cuckoo door surround (14) and the roof strips (15). Beneath the dial is a quatrefoil panel (16), and to either side a buttress (10). The drawings for most of these items are given on a squared background enlarged to make it easier for the reader to transfer the shape to the wood. All the carvings are executed in lime wood.

Dial surround and finials

Items which need woodturning are the dial surround (9) and the finials (18). The dial surround is rather thin so use the brown paper/scotch glue technique to fix this to the faceplate. For this first glue the lime wood disc to a backboard using a sheet of brown paper in between, and cramp this to hold it flat while the

106

glue is setting. Then screw fix the backboard to the faceplate. Next machine the dial surround and afterwards gently split the connection down the paper joint. The separation can be a little tricky particularly as the dial board is so thin, but the application of a knife and/or a little hot water will help you break the joint. Lastly spindle turn the finials and dowel fit these unglued into holes drilled in the bottom of the side buttresses (10).

Hands and numerals

On early cuckoo clocks up until 1860 carved bone hands were used, and after 1900 white plastic hands and numerals were fitted. If carved bone ones are attempted the initial sawing out I am told can be slightly smelly so be warned! Plastic hands and Roman gothic numerals are available in a range of sizes.

Movement

Of all the clock designs in this book this is probably the most difficult case to find a suitable movement. Cuckoo clock movements available today tend to be weight driven rather than spring powered as in this design. However, by strange coincidence I came across a photograph of an almost identical cuckoo clock case which was weight driven rather than spring powered, which suggests the clock was clearly being made in both variants during the last century. Thus a weight driven movement would be an acceptable solution, and it is relatively easy to adapt the casework to suit this by removing the bottom door and modifying the size of the opening to suit the disposition of the chains, weights and pendulum. The position of the cuckoo relative to the dial centre also might not align correctly with the cuckoo door opening and adjustment may be needed to the bird post accordingly. Check the limitations with the supplier first before you purchase the movement. The availability of accessories such as wind pipes, cuckoos, hands, numerals and pendulums generally seems to be better than for movements. See the list of suppliers for suitable sources.

Finish

A waxed finish is recommended for the case. To do this apply a shellac sealer followed by two rubbers of French polish. Wire wool down as necessary in between coats, and then vigorously wax the case taking care with the more fragile items.

PARTS LIST

Item	No	Material	Dimensions (mm)
Casework			
1 Side	1	Lime	135×12×305 long
2 Roof	2	Lime	195×10×220 long
3 Bottom	1	Lime	135×12×190 long
4 Front panel	1	Lime	212×10×520 long
5 Back panel	1	Spruce	190×10×360 long
6 Arch back panel	1	Lime	182×6×160 long
7 Side door	2	Lime	42×10×95 long
8 Bottom door	1	Lime	70×10×110 long
9 Dial panel	1	Lime	210×10×210 long. Woodturned to suit
10 Side buttress	2	Lime	60×10×210 long
11 Roof front gable	2	Lime	40×7×50 long
12 Roof side gable	2	Lime	60×10×110 long
13 Gable edge	2	Lime	14×6×170 long
14 Cuckoo door surround	1	Lime	75×6×100 long

15	Cuckoo door roof rail	2	Lime	16×4×65 long
16	Cuckoo door	2	Lime	16×6×60 long
17	Quatrefoil panel	1	Lime	110×6×220 long
18	Bottom finial	2	Lime	35sq×100 long

Movement & fittings

19	Hinge	6	Brass	Purchase to suit

20	Door catch	3	Brass	Make to detail
21	Dial numerals	1 set	White plastic	Roman gothic style. Purchase to suit
22	Hands	1 pair	White plastic	28 nominal height. Purchase to suit
23	Movement	1		Eight day cuckoo clock movement. Spring or weight driven

LONGCASE
CLOCKS

CHAPTER 15

Marquetry longcase clock
(c. 1685)

In the last few chapters of this book I am going to discuss the design of four English longcase clocks roughly in chronological order of time. Before starting with one of the earliest, a late seventeenth century marquetry clock, I will briefly describe the development of early longcase clock design to see how they were introduced.

In the formative years the first English longcase clocks produced about 1660 had rather severe simple lines, with an architectural roof top style and panelled oak casework veneered with ebony. These clock cases were narrow because short pendulums were being used, but lasted only briefly until full seconds pendulums were adopted as standard, when the casework became wider and better proportioned. About

1670 a new timber, walnut, was introduced which was popular for furniture for the next fifty years, and along with this the new technique of veneering was also introduced. Longcase clock design changed accordingly and highly decorated 'marquetry clocks' soon became fashionable. Fig 15.1 illustrates the principal styles in these early years. After the architectural style as in (A), parquetry veneering was introduced. These cases had regular geometric patterns such as stars, circles, ellipses, fan motifs and oyster squares (B). By 1680 clock makers had become more adventurous veneering the entire case front with 'bird and flower' patterns as in (C), the panels sometimes outlined with holly or ebony strings. Taken to extremes this resulted in the very fine 'seaweed'

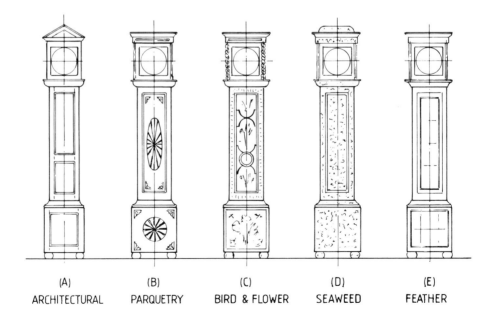

(A) ARCHITECTURAL   (B) PARQUETRY   (C) BIRD & FLOWER   (D) SEAWEED   (E) FEATHER

15.1 *Early longcase clock styles*

or arabesque marquetry (D). Subsequently the period 1710–1720 saw a return to plainer veneering and the application of feather banding (E).

In the Francis Legh collection at Lyme Park, N.T. which I have spoken of earlier in this book, there are a number of fine English longcase clocks representative of the walnut period and the styles mentioned above. There are two floral marquetry longcase clocks, one by Henry Young c.1675, the other by William Grimes c.1675, and a seaweed marquetry case by Christopher Gould c.1690 with a grand-sonnerie strike. There is also a notable Tompion longcase clock with a walnut case c.1700 having a Dutch strike and repeat, and a George Graham walnut longcase clock c.1735 with a deadbeat escapement. These were all London clock makers producing movements and cases of the highest quality.

Clock and movement

From the above I have selected the marquetry clock by William Grimes, London c.1685 as the first longcase clock design. This has a 250mm (10in) square brass dial with a matted centre, ringed winding holes and an engraved square calendar aperture. In the corners are cherub head pattern spandrels and the silvered chapter ring is signed 'Wm. Grimes, Londini Fecit'. The movement is of the latched pillar type and has an anchor escapement with a seconds pendulum. The hour striking movement now uses the rack and snail system but was originally designed for a count wheel.

The casework is oak and pine, veneered externally with walnut, and is crossbanded on the trunk front and sides. The marquetry work on the hood, trunk and base is interesting and depicts deer and hunting scenes in a variety of woods. The hood has a flat top with pierced fretwork above the dial, ebonized twisted columns, and glazed apertures on either side. The clock also has the early type of 'rising hood' which lifts up instead of sliding forward. Other typical period casework features are the convex moulding on the trunk below the hood, the glass lenticule and semi-elliptic lipping on the trunk door, and the ebonized bun feet. The convex style moulding only lasted for a short period and after about 1700 changed permanently to a concave shape. On very rare cases a lenticule is

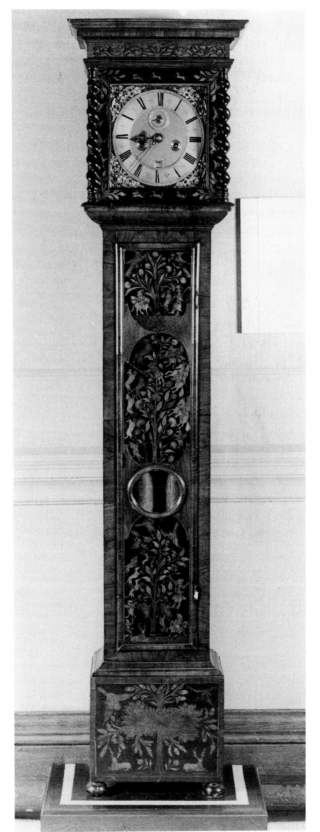

15.2 *Marquetry longcase clock*

occasionally seen in the base rather than the trunk but this is mainly associated with the 1¼ seconds beat pendulum which had a very long pendulum of 1554mm (61in).

15.3 *Dial plate of W. Grimes longcase clock*

15.4 *Trunk door marquetry hunting scenes*

Construction

The general arrangement is shown in Fig 15.6 and the sectional arrangement in Fig 15.7. Cross sections through the casework at various levels are given in Figs 15.8 and 15.9. Enlarged details of the hood and trunk door are shown in Fig 15.10. With regard to the original woods used, on some items this was difficult to verify due to limited access. For example it proved impossible to check the wood used for the base side panels which externally had a walnut veneer overlay and internally were hidden behind the extended sides of the trunk. In the parts list assumptions have been made based on knowledge of timbers used on other longcase clocks. While this clock seems to be made predominantly of oak perhaps because it is a quality London case, generally the ground on marquetry cases is more often pine.

15.5 *Base marquetry oak tree and deer scene*

Trunk

Commence construction by making the trunk which is a box construction comprising the sides (11), backboard (12), and cross rails (9) and

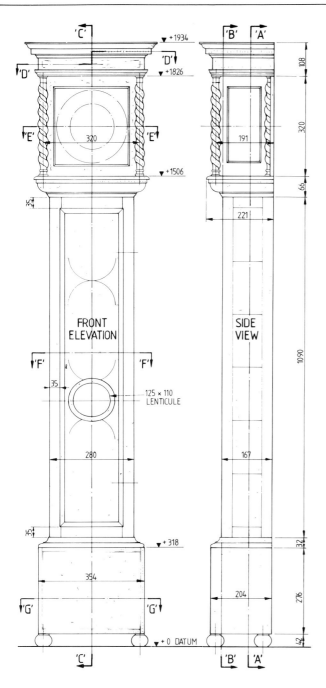

15.6 *General arrangement of marquetry longcase clock*

Base

With the trunk section completed apart from mouldings the next step is to add the base components, i.e. the front and sides. As mentioned above the trunk sides are carried through to the bottom of the case rather than stopped short just below the top of the base. This seems to be characteristic of these early clocks. On most longcase clocks the support between the trunk and the base is made solely by the moulding round the bottom of the trunk (i.e. item 3). I have always felt this to be a weak connection but there are thousands of clocks built like this so it seems to work. However, you may like to add an optional support strip (4). The next step is to close the back by adding the fill in strips (7), and fit corner strips (5) at the bottom of the base ready to support the bun feet. See enlarged detail in Fig 15.10. Finally woodturn the bun feet, ebonize them, and fit these to the base with dowels.

Hood

The principal hood items are the side panels (23), fascia (27), soffit (28), dial front framework (24), roof support strip (26) and the roof board (31). The latter is an important item serving to stabilize and square up the hood, and you therefore need to work around this as the structure is built up. The following is the suggested order of work.

First, prepare all the major items above to the dimensions given, leaving a little spare material on the ends of rails and strip work where appropriate for later trimming. Make each hood side, by cutting out the glazed aperture, and gluing on fascia (27), and then indent these ready to fit items (24), (26) and (29). Start the hood assembly by first gluing and pinning each hood side/fascia onto the roof board (31). Next glue the roof support strip (26) in place, and the remaining section of the fascia strip (27) across the front. It may be easier at this stage to work with the hood roof face down on the bench ready to accept other items. Make up the dial framework (24), which is a half jointed assembly, and fix this to the front of the hood. Complete the top section of the hood by gluing on the soffit (28) with additional pinning if necessary, and lastly add the mouldings (32), (33) and (34).

(10). The backboard extends across the full width of the trunk and is glued and pinned to the sides from behind Form the trunk door framework by letting cross rails (9) into the sides at top and bottom, and fitting stile strips (8) either side. Leave the sides over long at the top so that the seatboard can be positioned correctly later.

113

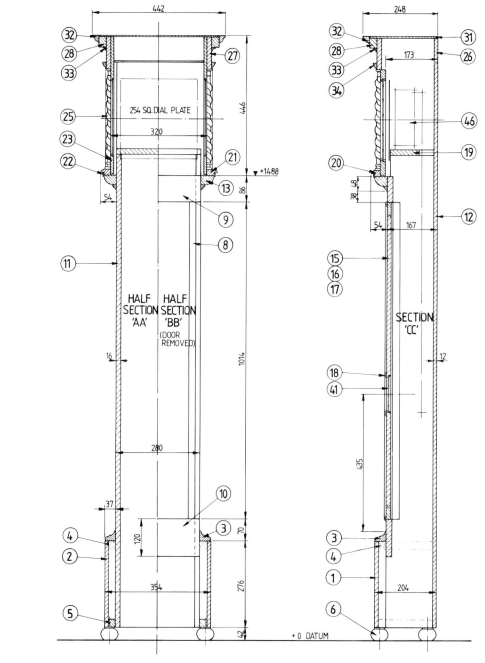

15.7 *Sectional arrangement of marquetry longcase clock*

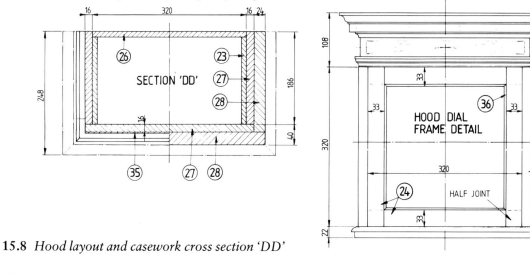

15.8 *Hood layout and casework cross section 'DD'*

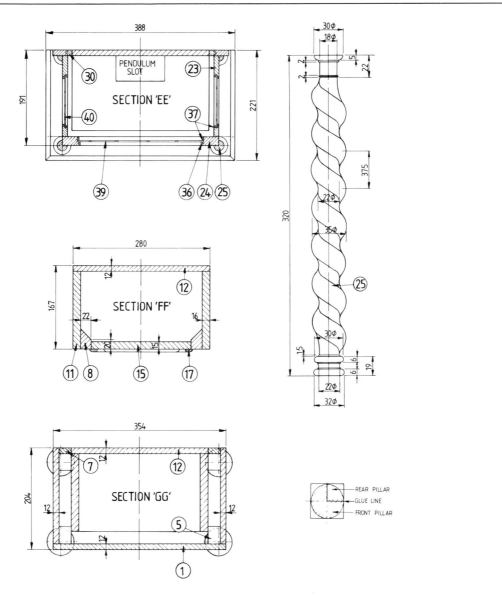

15.9 *Casework cross sections*

Details of the pierced fretwork are shown in Fig 15.10 on a squared background to aid transfer to the wood. Cut this out with a fretsaw fitted with a fine tooth blade which will minimize finishing work. Fit the fretwork panel across the hood fascia with a pale blue silk backing behind. Drill a series of 2.5mm holes through the fascia over which the fret is fitted to make it easier for the hour strike to be heard. Round the base of the hood is a moulded ledge rail (items 20 and 21) which you should glue fix to place. Inset this with a register (22) to locate the hood to the trunk top moulding. The hood is supported off the trunk by an upper moulding (13). This is of convex form comprising a thin strip of walnut over a pine base glue fixed to the trunk case.

Rising hood motion

As explained earlier the hood on this clock is lifted to gain access to the dial for winding. This slides on a tongue and groove feature fitted at the back of the case. The splats (29) which are glue fixed to the hood have a vertical groove cut in them, and these slide over a tongued guide strip (30) fixed to the edges of the backboard (see Fig 15.10 section 'EE'). To stop the hood dropping whilst the clock is being wound a spring steel latch is screw fixed to the backboard. When the hood is lifted, the latch springs out under the bottom edge of the ledge rail/side. You release the catch by pushing it in clear of the side and gently lower the hood. Fig 15.11 shows a typical spoon latch.

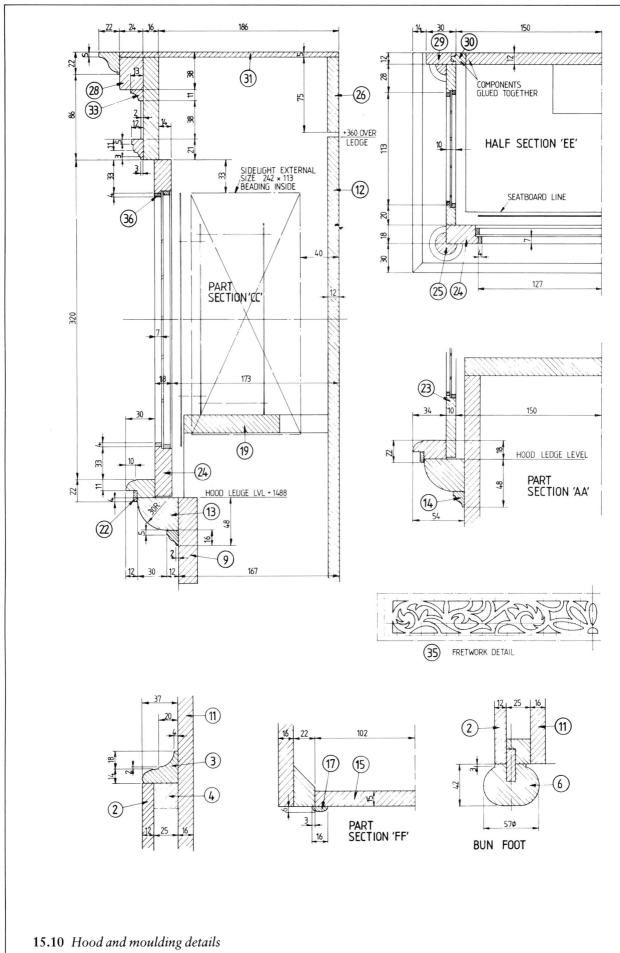

15.10 *Hood and moulding details*

machining, and ensure that you wear a protective visor for this operation. When you have finished machining, mark out the plain turned middle section ready for the barley twist and then carve this out. When this is complete unscrew the items and part them by applying heat and/or hot water to the joint. Pear wood is proposed for the pillars which besides being a good carvers wood was commonly used by clock makers where an ebonized finish was required.

Trunk door

Make the trunk door from a vertical oak board and fit a horizontal rail across the top and bottom. On early clocks these rails were often plain butt jointed which is not a good way of doing things, and it is suggested that you fit these to the door panel using a stopped tongue and groove joint which will minimize warping. There can be problems with the external veneer crazing at the joint with this type of construction (see Fig 18.11). In the middle of the door is an oval lenticule, but round ones were also fitted on these early cases and this might be easier to make. Fix the glass in the lenticule with brown coloured putty. Round the edge of the lenticule and the trunk door perimeter is an elliptic section cross-grained walnut lipping. Mount the door on longcase pattern strap hinges as shown in Fig 15.12. These have a pivot point slightly forward of the front face of the trunk door, so that the door bead or lipping does not foul the trunk when opened.

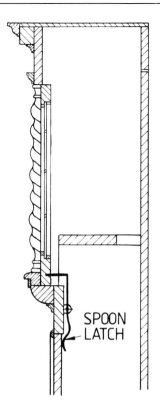

15.11 *Hood locking lever detail*

Although not authentic with the period you may prefer to fit a front opening door rather than a rising hood to make access for winding a little easier. If this is done I suggest that you fit a dial mask to strengthen the front of the hood, referring to other longcase clock designs in this book for details. I have seen a Tompion longcase clock of this period modified in this way.

Barley twist columns

Either side of the hood is a barley twist pillar fitted at each corner of the front dial frame (24), and also a quarter section twist glued to the back splats (29) (see section 'EE', Fig 15.10). At first sight these might seem especially difficult to make, but actually it is rather easier than it looks and the method is as follows.

First prepare square section timber for the main pillar (42mm sq) and the quarter column (21mm sq). Next cut out a corner section of the main pillar and glue in the quarter pillar as shown in Fig 15.9 section 'EE', using paper and scotch glue. Then mount this assembly on the lathe ready for woodturning. For additional protection screw the two parts together at either end to minimize the risk of the separation during

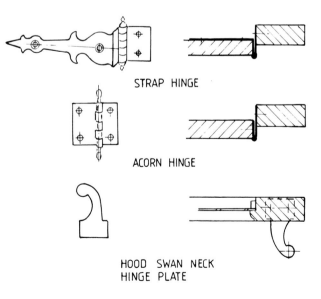

15.12 *Longcase clock hood and trunk door hinges*

Veneering

The general aspect of veneering is very much a personal choice. Obviously the marquetry as shown in Figs 15.4 and 15.5 requires a certain degree of skill in this craft, but there are alternative choices as mentioned under the notes on case styles discussed earlier. Parquetry is a simpler option and you could also use plainer book matched walnut veneers.

Movement and dial

Fit an eight day weight driven longcase clock movement striking on a bell. This should be of the best quality possible fitted with a 250mm square brass dial plate, chapter ring and corner spandrels. Some general notes on the assembly of longcase dial plates and movements covering the methods of mounting and fixing dial plates, chapter rings and spandrels are given on pp. 126–28.

PARTS LIST

Item	No	Material	Dimensions (mm)
Base			
1 Base front	1	Oak	276×12×354 long
2 Base side	2	Oak	204×12×276 long
3 Base top moulding	1	Walnut/ pine	37×32×800 long total. Walnut edging over pine base
4 Support strip	1	Oak	25sq×760 long total Optional fitting
5 Corner strip	4	Oak	25sq×35 long
6 Bun foot	4	Pear	65sq×60 long
7 Back strip	2	Pine	25×12×276 long
Trunk			
8 Stile strip	2	Oak	42×22×1014 long
9 Cross rail (1)	1	Oak	86×20×280 long
10 Cross rail (2)	1	Oak	120×20×280 long
11 Trunk side	2	Oak	167×16× 1520 long
12 Back board	1	Pine	280×12× 1806 long
13 Trunk top moulding (1)	1	Walnut/ pine	42×32×800 long total. Walnut edging over pine base
14 Trunk top moulding (2)	1	Walnut	16×12×700 long total
15 Door	1	Oak	204×15×924 long
16 Door top/ bottom rail	2	Oak	45×15×204 long
17 Door edge moulding	1	Walnut	16×6×1500 long
18 Lenticule moulding	1	Walnut	Make to suit
19 Seat board	1	Pine	150×18×280 long
Hood			
20 Front rail	1	Walnut	30×18×388 long
21 Side rail	2	Walnut	34×18×221 long
22 Register strip	1	Walnut	12×4×840 long total
23 Hood side panel	2	Oak	161×10×442 long. Consider changing to walnut
24 Hood dial frame strip	4	Oak	33×18×320 long. Walnut veneered
25 Barley twist pillar	2	Pear	42sq×370 long & 21sq×370 long. See script
26 Roof support strip	1	Pine	75×12×320 long
27 Fascia	1	Pine	108×16×750 long total
28 Soffit	1	Pine	38×24×820 long total

29	Splat strip	2	Walnut	30×12×360 long
30	Guide strip	2	Pine	15×12×360 long
31	Roof board	1	Oak	226×5×398 long
32	Hood moulding (1)	1	Walnut	22sq×960 long total
33	Hood moulding (2)	1	Walnut	13×11×850 long total
34	Hood moulding (3)	1	Walnut	21×12×850 long total
35	Fretwork panel	1	Walnut	38×2×352 long
36	Beading (external)	1	Walnut	4×7×2700 long total
37	Beading (internal)	1	Oak	4×7×2700 long total
38	Veneer & crossbanding	–	Walnut	Veneer all over case

Glass

39	Door glass	1	Picture glass	258sq
40	Sidelight	2	Picture glass	244×115
41	Lenticule	1	Picture glass.	Oval cut to suit opening

Metalwork

42	Trunk door hinge	2	Brass	Longcase pattern Purchase to suit
43	Escutcheon	1	Brass	Purchase to suit
44	Lock	1	Brass	Purchase to suit
45	Dial/ spandrels	1	Brass	254sq nominal
46	Movement/ pendulum	1	–	Eight day movement c/w seconds pendulum
47	Minute/hour hand	1 pr	–	Purchase to suit
48	Silk	1	Blue silk	Cut to suit

CHAPTER 16

Lancashire longcase clock
(c.1770)

While early longcase clocks were mostly produced by specialist clock makers in London or the home counties, provincial craftsmen were not slow to take up the challenge, and by the mid-eighteenth century a wide diversity were being made throughout Britain. Country longcase clocks were often made by village craftsmen as a sideline to their many other products, and in the larger towns and cities clock makers were busy working to meet the public demand. As the production of longcase clocks spread throughout the country it was only natural that regional variations should develop, and an experienced horologist is able to tell with some confidence from which part of Britain one may have originated.

An example of a mid-eighteenth century regional clock is the Lancashire longcase in Fig 16.1. This has typical North West country features with oak casework, cross banding on the hood, trunk and base, a caddy top and ogee feet. On the hood above the dial is a characteristic Lancashire feature, a decorated glass strip gold painted on a black background. Inspection of the dial signed 'Thomas Clare, Warrington' reveals the direct indication of its origin. The dial is one handed, having an hour hand but no minute hand, and the spandrel pattern is 'two birds with urn' a style common between 1735–60. If you think about it when this clock was made during the eighteenth century, the passage of time was not regulated as rigidly as it is today. There were no trains to catch, and the timetable for travel by horse and carriage must have been somewhat irregular. The need for a minute hand was hence relatively unimportant. Nonetheless with a little bit of practice you can tell the time on a single handed clock to within about five or ten minutes. By

inspection of the dial plate (Fig. 16.2) you can also see immediately that a 30 hour movement is fitted for there are no winding holes. If an eight day movement was fitted then there would be visible winding holes through the dial plate. On a 30 hour movement the weights are rewound by a rope or chain system access to which is obtained by opening the trunk door. Usually a Huygen's endless chain system is employed to provide maintaining power while being rewound. Otherwise the clock would lose time say a minute per rewind and after a week could easily be as much as 5–10 minutes slow.

Construction

The general arrangement of the longcase clock is shown in Fig 16.6 with sectional details in Fig 16.7. In addition Figs 16.8 and 16.9 detail the hood profile and a number of cross sections at various levels through the clock. Enlarged details of the hood, mouldings and are given in Fig 16.10 and details of the ogee feet in Fig 16.10. The suggested order of construction is first the trunk, then the base and last the hood.

Trunk

The trunk is a simple box section comprising the sides (15), backboard (3), and the door framework (12), (13) and (14). Butt joint the sides and back adding fillet reinforcement at the corners. Joint the door framework with mortice and tenons and rebate the stiles to fit the sides. Form the beaded corners on the stiles using a scratch stock. Make the top rail with a wavy edge profile to match the trunk door.

16.2 *Thomas Clare dial plate*

16.3 *Painted glass panel on hood*

16.4 *Ogee foot detail*

16.1 *Lancashire longcase clock*

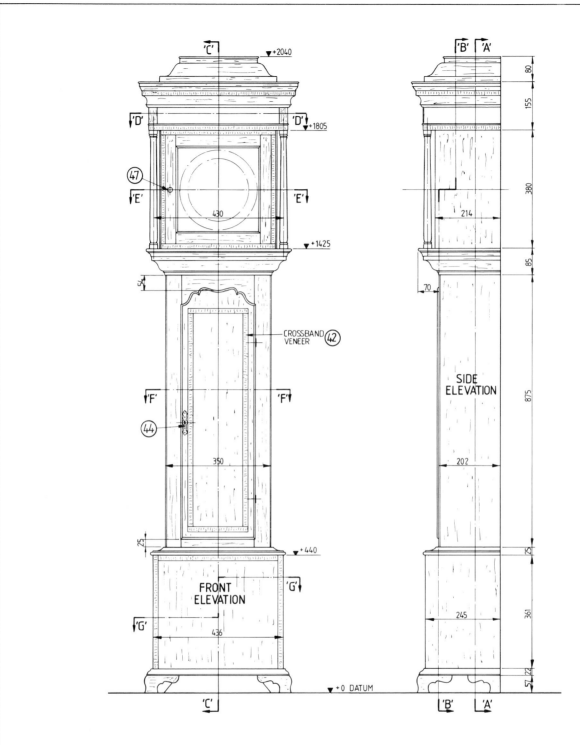

16.5 (Below) *Trunk door profile*

16.6 (Above) *General arrangement of Lancashire longcase clock*

Base

The original base construction puzzled me for a while, but after study I concluded that the sides were solid oak with vertical grain, whilst the front was possibly pine with an oak veneer face. The front panel was laid traditionally with the grain the longest way in this instance across the base (see Fig 18.14). I think if I was making it

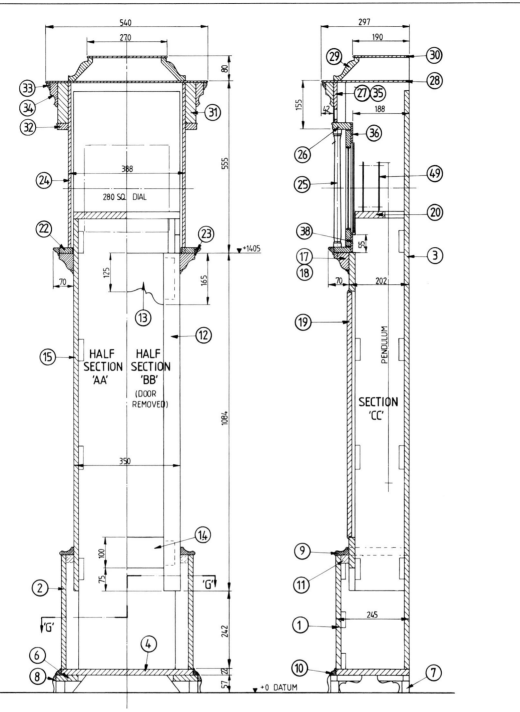

16.7 *Sectional arrangement of Lancashire longcase*

again I would be tempted to fit a quarter sawn
oak panel in two or three vertical strips to
minimise wood movement and avoid the
complication of veneering the base front. In
Chapter 18 there is a summary of the principles
of base construction and the associated
problems of wood movement. Lastly I would
mention that the original base has a bottom
which is relatively uncommon on longcase

clocks most being left open.

Proceeding with the base construction as per
drawing, first make the front and sides and
rebate and glue them together. Then add on the
bottom to square the assembly and pin this from
the underside. Next prepare the mouldings (9)
and (10) and fit these to the case. Moulding (9)
connects the base to the trunk, and moulding
(10) conceals the edge of the bottom (4). An
optional trunk support strip (11) may make it
easier to join the trunk and base together.
Finally make and fit the ogee feet items (6), (7)

16.8 (Below) *Casework cross sections*

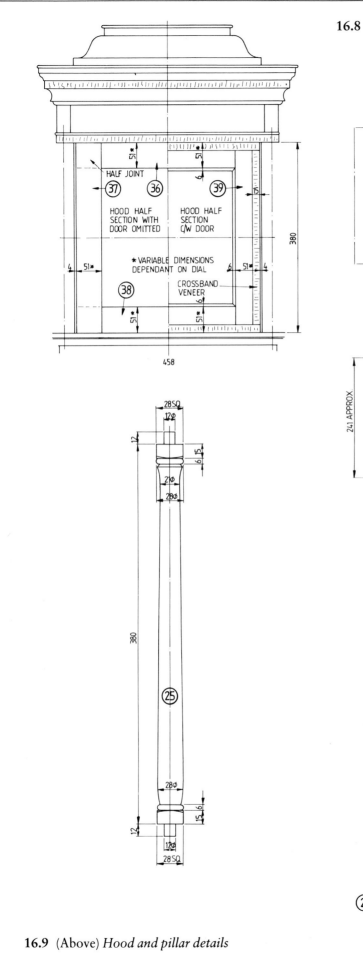

HALF JOINT
(37) (36) (39)

HOOD HALF
SECTION WITH
DOOR OMITTED

HOOD HALF
SECTION
C/W DOOR

* VARIABLE DIMENSIONS
DEPENDANT ON DIAL

(38)

CROSSBAND
VENEER

458

28 SQ
12∅

(25)

28∅

28 SQ

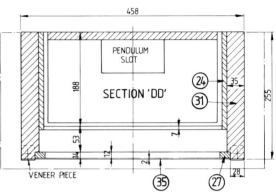

458

PENDULUM
SLOT

SECTION 'DD'

(24)
(31)

VENEER PIECE

(35) (27)

255

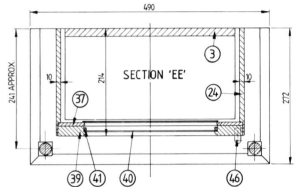

490

(3)

SECTION 'EE'

(37) (24)

241 APPROX

272

(39) (41) (40) (46)

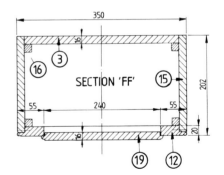

350

(3)
(16)

SECTION 'FF'

(15)

55 240 55

202

(19) (12)

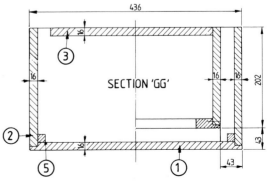

436

(3)

16

SECTION 'GG'

16 16

202

(2)

(5) (1)

43

16.9 (Above) *Hood and pillar details*

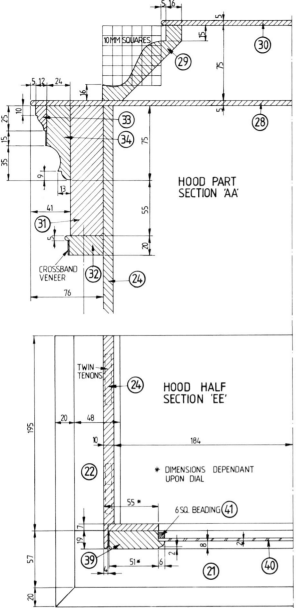

16.10 *Hood and trunk door sections*

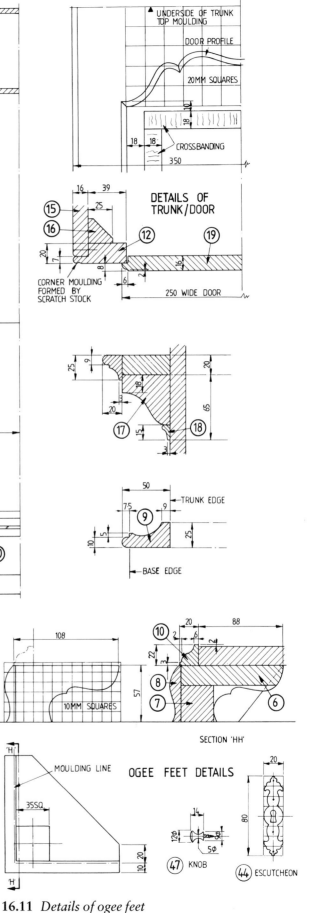

and (8). An alternative method of fixing the backboard (3) to the base is to extend it down over the edge of the bottom (4) the latter being cut back to suit. The back is then screw fixed to the bottom from behind. Finally make the mouldings at the top of the trunk, items (17) and (18) and fit these ready to support the hood.

Trunk door

The trunk door is of one piece construction and ideally you should make this from quarter sawn oak to minimize warping. Form the beaded edge surround either by machine routing or by a scratchstock. The wavy top form with re-entrant

16.11 *Details of ogee feet*

corners either side is a common shape found on longcase clocks extending over a long period of time. The door profile is shown in Figs 16.5 and 16.11. Pivot the door on strap hinges and fit it with a suitable lock and escutcheon.

Hood frame

The hood construction is given in Figs 16.9 and 16.10. The basic structure consists of support rails (21) and (22), hood side panels (24), a roof board (28), and a mask framework (36), (37) and (38). Make these items and then assemble and glue them together. Stiffen this up with additional strips and mouldings as indicated. Half joint the support rails together and tenon the side panels (24) into these. Also make the pine mask framework which again is a half jointed assembly, and fit this into a rebate cut in the front edges of the side panels. This frame will help to square up the hood. Above the mask is a soffit (26) half jointed at the corners with the side soffits (32), the former fitting into a small cut out in the hood sides. Over the soffit is a fascia comprising items (27) and (31). Rebate these together at the corners and glue item (31) onto the hood sides. Finally make the roof board (28) and glue/pin this on with fascia mouldings (33) and (34) previously prepared.

Miscellaneous hood items

A few items still remain to be added to the hood. These are the pillars, the caddy top, the painted glass strip and the hood door. The side pillars are simple woodturned items. These are shown with optional spigot ends but on the original clock the pillars are just a tight glued fit into the space between the support rail (21) and the front soffit (26). If you make the pillars with spigot ends then you will need to modify the hood assembly order to accommodate this. The caddy top consists of an ogee section item (29) and caddy roof board (30) glued together. This is an optional item and if there are height restrictions can be omitted. Next you should cut the decorated glass strip which fits on the fascia over the dial. After fitting this remove it temporarily to paint the gold/black pattern on the back. Alternatively you could fit a fretted panel with silk backing similar to the marquetry clock in Chapter 15.

Hood door

The hood door is a simple framework half jointed at the corners and rebated to fit the glass. The frame has a quarter radius bead outside facing the glass and the latter is held in place internally with square beading pinned to place. The door pivots externally on two brass plate hinges (46) which are usually supplied undrilled. Drill and screw fix these to the top and bottom edges of the door frame (Fig 16.9 Section EE). Fit a brass door knob to suit. An alternative hood door construction occasionally seen on country clocks is one with a mitred corner as in Fig 16.12 and has a thin wood strip insert fitted across the corner. This is slightly more fussy to make requiring an accurate mitre connection. The half jointed door frame is by far the easiest to make which is why it predominates on longcase clocks. Hoods were sometimes fitted with a locking device as illustrated in Fig 16.12. This consists of a simple wood catch screwed to the inside of the trunk which twists and locks into a tongue projection fixed to the bottom of the hood door. This catch has the advantage not only of locking the hood door closed, but also prevents the hood itself from accidentally sliding forward.

Crossband veneering

The extent of the oak crossbanding is shown on the general arrangement and Fig 16.4. Sometimes mahogany crossbanding was used to contrast with the oak casework.

Movement and dial

In general a longcase clock is fitted with an eight day weight driven movement with a seconds pendulum and an hour strike facility. There are a wide selection available but it is not always easy to make the right choice. The Lancashire longcase here is designed to suit a movement fitted with a 280mm square dial plate which is a size commonly available. In Chapter 3 I discussed the way dials and movements are fixed to bracket clock casework. Their application to longcase clocks is similar though there are differences, so I thought I would summarize these here together with some general points on how these fit together. This

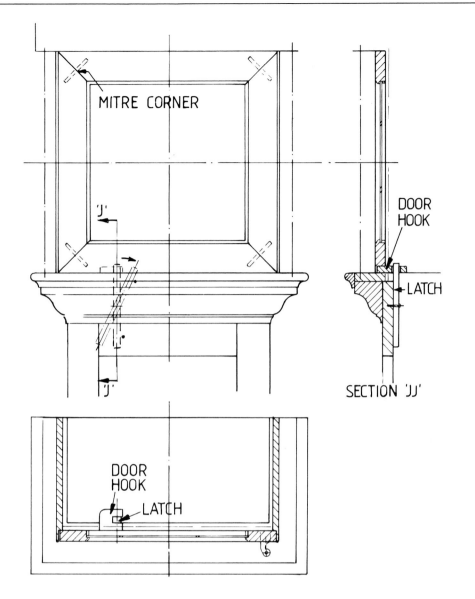

16.12 *Mitre hood door construction and latch mechanism*

varies slightly in relation movements fitted to period clocks and modern day equivalents, and I will highlight the differences.

Dials

In a period longcase clock the dial is composed of three items, the dial plate, chapter ring and spandrels as shown in Fig 16.13. The dial plate is the main component which is connected to the movement, and it also serves to carry the chapter ring and spandrels.

The chapter ring is an annular brass plate usually about 50–60mm wide fixed to the front of the dial plate, on which is engraved the hour divisions, minute ring and Roman numerals.

This ring is silvered on the front face and the engravings are filled with black wax. The chapter ring has a number of small pegs riveted to the back of it. These pass through matching holes in the dial plate and are fixed behind by a taper pin fitting through a hole in the end as shown in Fig 16.13. The pegs are often in the 3 o'clock, 6 o'clock, 9 o'clock and 12 o'clock positions but may vary to suit individual dial plates.

Spandrels are decorative brass castings which surround the chapter ring and fit in the corners of the dial plate filling this empty space. All sorts of spandrel patterns were produced over the years, and knowledge of the styles can help you to date a clock. They are commonly fixed either by screws and rivets, or the peg and pin method described above. Spandrels should be a nice bright brass colour and not have an 'antiqued' finish as provided by some suppliers. They should also be purchased in a pattern to suit the stylistic period of the clock you are making.

The dial plate itself is a large square piece of thick brass plate with or without an arch section, and is 'posted' to the movement by means of a number of short brass pillars. These pillars (commonly four) are riveted to the back of the dial plate and the shouldered ends pass through the front plate of the movement, and are fixed behind by a transverse pin similar to how the chapter ring is secured. The pillars are usually positioned behind the chapter ring so that they are not visible from the front of the dial. After the hands are added, the complete unit comprising the dial plate/movement is then placed on the seatboard, to which the latter is then secured. Methods of securing movements to seatboards are as for bracket clocks (see Fig 3.9).

Looking now at modern day longcase clock dials and movements made for the mass market, you will more likely find these provided as separate entities which are fixed independently to the case. Very often there is no provision to post the dial and movement together, and the dial plate may be supplied complete with spandrels and chapter ring already fitted. On cheaper arrangements the chapter ring and spandrels may simply be stuck onto the dial plate instead of being fixed with rivets, pins or screws. With regard to the dial plate itself, this is usually fixed by small pins or screws through small holes in the perimeter onto a solid board mask behind. Again some cheap dial plates may not even have this provision and are simply stuck on. It may still be possible though to fix the dial plate in the conventional manner, i.e. into a mask frame from behind provide a rebate is machined in this to suit. Additionally you may also find that on cheaper chapter rings the material is aluminium (with printed numerals) instead of brass, and as just mentioned the spandrels could be 'antiqued'. With regard to securing the movement this may be by brackets to the case backboard rather than the normal seatboard fixture.

So which way should you do it? The answer depends on how periodically correct you want your clock to be, and to a degree how much you are prepared to spend. If this does not concern you, then you can purchase one of the cheaper standard dial plate assemblies and fit this. You could however consider a small improvement by removing any antique finish on the spandrels to reveal the native brass beneath, and then lacquer these to stop them tarnishing. The other option, and to my mind the better one, is to make up a dial plate assembly from individually made components which are periodically correct. These are available made in the proper materials and with the correct fixtures, but you may have to pay a little more for them.

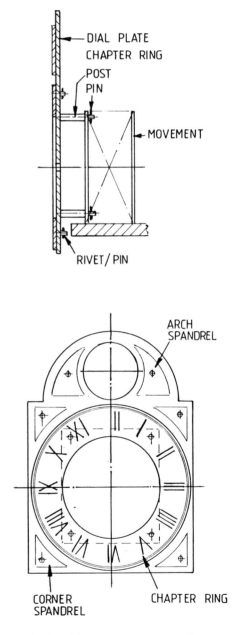

16.13 *Methods of fixing movements to longcase clocks*

which is compatible with the period style of the clock you are making. This is not always easy, partly because today there is a strong emphasis on longcase clock movements made to strike on rod gongs and tubes rather than bells. These are often fitted with triple chime arrangements such as Westminster, Whittington and St. Michael, which are relatively modern innovations dating post 1850. If you are reproducing the Lancashire longcase clock for example in the style of the original c.1770 then you should aim to fit a movement which strikes on a bell. Sources for longcase movements which strike on bells are given in the list of suppliers. Although most of these are continental there are still clock makers in England who specialize in producing these.

Setting up

There are two aspects to setting up a movement. One is the matter of pendulum swing, and the other the alignment of the dial plate into the mask. The alignment into the mask is easily adjusted by setting the seatboard at the correct height. With regard to pendulum swing suppliers usually quote this 'overall' including the specified pendulum bob proposed as shown in Fig 16.14. If the size of the pendulum bob is changed then the swing changes accordingly. The swing should of course be less than the internal trunk width, and you should allow a good margin either side.

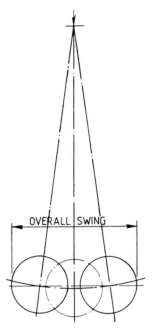

PENDULUM SWING

16.14 *Pendulum swing*

Movements, strikes and chimes

In Chapter 1 I briefly discussed the question of movement selection and what to look for when buying one. I also mentioned a number of strikes and chimes but not which type you should fit. What you should aim to do is to choose one

PARTS LIST

Item	No	Material	Dimensions (mm)
Base			
1 Base front	1	Oak	436×16×363 long
2 Base side	2	Oak	245×16×363 long
3 Back board	1	Pine	318×16×1850 long
4 Bottom	1	Pine	245×20×436 long
5 Corner fillet (1)	1	Pine	15sq×500 long total
6 Support pad	4	Oak	120×19×360 long total
7 Support block	4	Oak	35sq×180 long total
8 Ogee foot moulding	8	Oak	57×12×120 long
9 Base top moulding	1	Oak	50×25×980 long
10 Base edge moulding	1	Oak	22×20×1050 long
11 Trunk support strip	1	Oak	27sq×1700 long total

Trunk

12	Stile	2	Oak	52×20×1084 long
13	Cross rail (1)	1	Oak	165×20×350 long
14	Cross rail (2)	1	Oak	100×20×350 long
15	Trunk side	2	Oak	202×16×1200 long
16	Corner fillet (2)	1	Pine	15sq×1100 long total
17	Trunk top moulding (1)	1	Oak	50sq×1000 long total
18	Trunk top moulding (2)	1	Oak	15×9×82 long total
19	Trunk door	1	Oak	250×16×805 long
20	Seat board	1	Pine	165×22×350 long

Hood

21	Front rail	1	Oak	57×20×450 long
22	Side rail	2	Oak	48×20×250 long
23	Rail edge moulding	1	Oak	25×20×1050 long
24	Hood side panel	2	Oak	214×10×550 long.
25	Pillar	2	Oak	35sq×435 long
26	Front soffit	1	Oak	65×20×465 long
27	Front fascia board	1	Oak	130×12×402 long
28	Roof board	1	Oak	297×5×540 long
29	Ogee roof moulding	1	Oak	120×28×1000 long total
30	Caddy roof board	1	Oak	190×5×270 long
31	Side fascia	2	Oak	130×35×255 long
32	Side soffit	2	Oak	40×20×260 long
33	Hood moulding (1)	1	Oak	25×12×1200 long total
34	Hood moulding (2)	1	Oak	75×24×1150 long total
35	Painted glass panel	1	Picture glass	55×402 long
36	Mask top strip	1	Pine	70×7×380 long
37	Mask side strip	2	Pine	51×7×420 long
38	Mask bottom strip	1	Pine	70×7×380 long
39	Hood door frame	4	Oak	57×19×380 long
40	Door glass	1	Picture glass	277sq. Cut to suit
41	Beading	1	Oak	6sq×1150 long total
42	Crossbanding	–	Oak	Alternatively mahogany. Quantity to suit

Metalwork

43	Trunk door hinge	2	Brass	Longcase pattern
44	Escutcheon	1	Brass	Purchase to suit
45	Lock	1	Brass	Purchase to suit
46	Hood door pivot	2	Brass	15×30 strip screw fixed
47	Door knob	1	Brass	12 nominal dia. Purchase to suit

Movement & dial

48	Dial/chapter ring/ spandrels	1	Brass	280sq nominal size. Purchase complete or make to suit
49	Movement/ pendulum	1	–	Eight day weight driven movement c/w seconds pendulum striking on a bell
50	Minute/hour hand	1 pair	Blued steel	Purchase to suit

CHAPTER 17

Pagoda longcase clock
(c.1780)

If I had to pick one style to symbolise elegance and grandeur in a longcase clock I think it would be the 'London' pagoda. This has a distinctive style of its own that is instantly recognisable (Fig 17.1) which sets it apart from a provincial equivalent. It is a tall dignified clock with a concave upswept hood, an arch dial, a well proportioned case with a long trunk, and a panelled double plinth base. It is generally fitted with high quality movements, dial plates and other special features, and the casework is characteristically veneered on the trunk and base with the finest curl mahogany.

Case features

The design is measured from a London longcase c.1780. In the description which follows which is specifically of this case, it should be noted that this is typical of this style of clock.

The pagoda hood is designed to accommodate an arched dial plate, which is framed by a broken arch style moulding over the dial, and 'double reeded' pillars either side with brass capitals top and bottom. There are plainer quarter pillars on the side splats, and glazed apertures in the sides. A further indicator of quality is the arched door which is mounted on side pattern hinges and fitted with a key lock. This compares with most other longcase hood doors which are hinged on plates and have only simple locking devices if any. The pagoda section above the arch is topped by a brass 'ball and spire' finial either side, below which is a vertical reeded moulding, and in the centre there is a distinctive pierced fret.

The trunk is long typically about a metre, and has 'double reeded' quarter columns either side

with brass capitals either end. The double reed effect is achieved by first grooving the columns, and then fitting brass strips in each flute at the bottom for about a third of the way up. The trunk door has a broken arch top and is inset with a moulded edge surround and fitted with a key lock. The base has a panelled front with radiused corner cut outs and a moulded edge surround similar to the trunk door. The case stands on a characteristic double plinth arrangement the front of which has a curved profile. Trunk and base are veneered with fine curl mahogany of good patination, and the hood door is crossbanded.

Dial and movement

Dial plate is nominally 305mm square with a silent/strike feature in the arch, and is fitted with an eight day five pillar movement. The matted centre has a seconds ring above the middle and a square date aperture below. In the corners are 'branch' pattern spandrels surrounding the silvered chapter ring which is marked with both Roman and Arabic numerals. This is complemented by a fine pair of pierced hands. The dial plate is signed 'Robert Ward, London' on a silvered arch crescent below the centre.

Construction

The general arrangement is shown in Fig 17.5 with principal sections in Fig 17.6. Cross sections at various levels through the clock and hood layout details are given in Figs 17.7 and 17.8. Enlarged details of the hood and mouldings are shown in Fig 17.9 and 17.10. The

17.2 *Dial from Robert Ward longcase*

17.3 *Pagoda top fretwork*

17.4 *Pagoda clock base*

17.1 *London pagoda longcase clock*

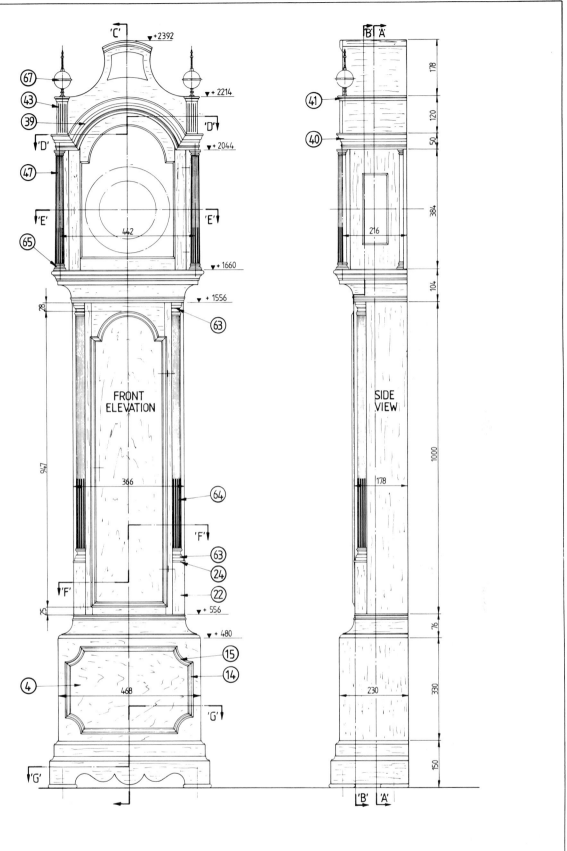

17.5 *General arrangement of pagoda longcase clock*

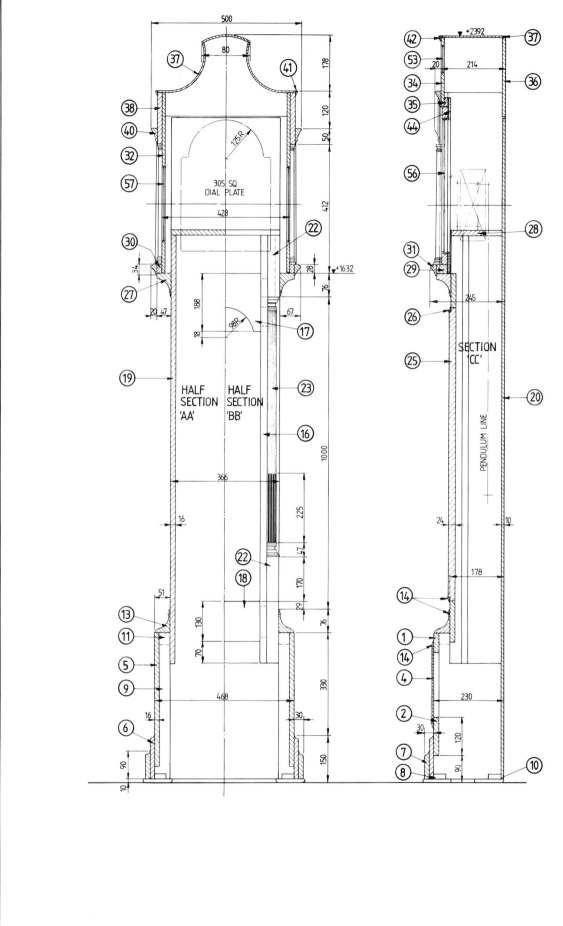

17.6 *Sectional arrangement of pagoda longcase clock*

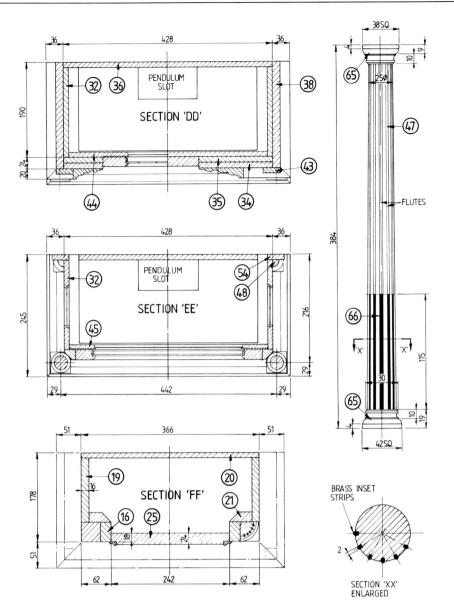

17.7 *Cross sections through casework*

base framework and pierced fret are detailed in Fig 17.11.

In previous chapters I have described in some detail the construction of two longcase clocks, and much of that comment is applicable to this longcase. It is not proposed therefore to discuss this in any great detail apart from constructional aspects specific to this clock, and the reader is referred to these chapters for more detailed general information.

One feature you will have to bear in mind before commencing construction is the height. This particular clock is taller than most and can be difficult to accommodate in a modern house with limited ceiling height which is commonly about 2.2–2.4m (8ft). Sometimes pagodas also

had a third ball and spire finial in the centre which aggravates the problem even more. It may be necessary to jiggle a bit here and there to make it so it will fit your rooms. Pagoda clock cases were made primarily in mahogany though oak was used sometimes for the trunk door and other less visible components.

Trunk

This is of conventional box construction with a trunk framework to accommodate the door. The rails (17) and (18) are shown morticed and tenoned to the stiles (16) though I was unable to verify this due to the veneer covering. It is

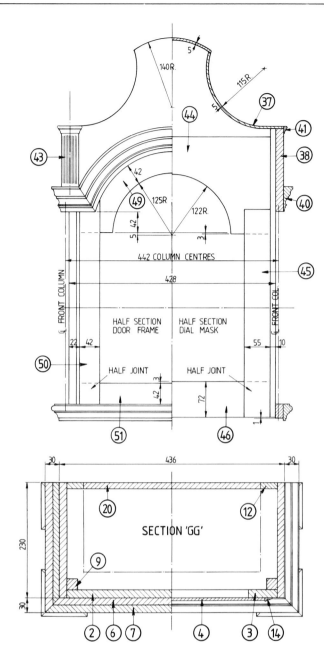

17.8 *Hood layout and section 'GG'*

perfectly possible they could in fact be simply set into cut outs in the stiles. The trunk is completed by miscellaneous strip work in the corners ready to accept the quarter columns.

Quarter columns

Make the quarter columns using an adaption of the method for making split columns described in Chapter 15 (barley twist columns). The difference here is that you need to glue together

three pieces of wood as shown in Fig 17.10, the larger piece subsequently being discarded when the joints are broken. Cut the flutes after woodturning and prior to breaking the joints. These will require machine routing and you will need to construct a suitable jig to do this. One suggestion is to make a box framework to hold the quarter column on its ends with provision along its length for a sliding router as shown in Fig 17.12. The details are left to the reader. A click stop feature for indexing the quarter columns round in incremental steps is recommended, and provision to firmly clamp this should be incorporated. There is nothing more frustrating than a row of machined wandering grooves! Finally fit the brass reed inserts. In the original these are made from pressed brass strip bent over at the top ends, but it is probably easier to cut and fit solid brass reeds.

Base

The base differs from earlier longcase clock designs in that the front is a framed mortice and tenon construction (Fig 17.11) rather than a one piece panel. The centre panel (14) has an edge moulding (14) which is used elsewhere on the case, i.e. trunk top and bottom mouldings and trunk door perimeter. Mount the base on a double plinth arrangement, and machine a scotia profile on the top edge of the plinth rails. Otherwise follow the construction used on previous longcase bases.

Hood

The hood construction is similar in many aspects to the Lancashire longcase clock in Chapter 16, except that the sides (32) are extended above the side moulding (40) and the pagoda top is then built up around this. Lay the roof in segmental strips and cover this with black paper glued on to finish. The pierced fret is shown on a squared background to aid transfer to the wood. Another alternative you could do is to make a basket weave panel for this opening. If you want to see what this looks like visit the Lady Lever Art Gallery near Liverpool, where there is a fine pagoda clock with this detail. Next make the fluted hood pillars (47) and the quarter pillars (48) in a similar manner described earlier. While

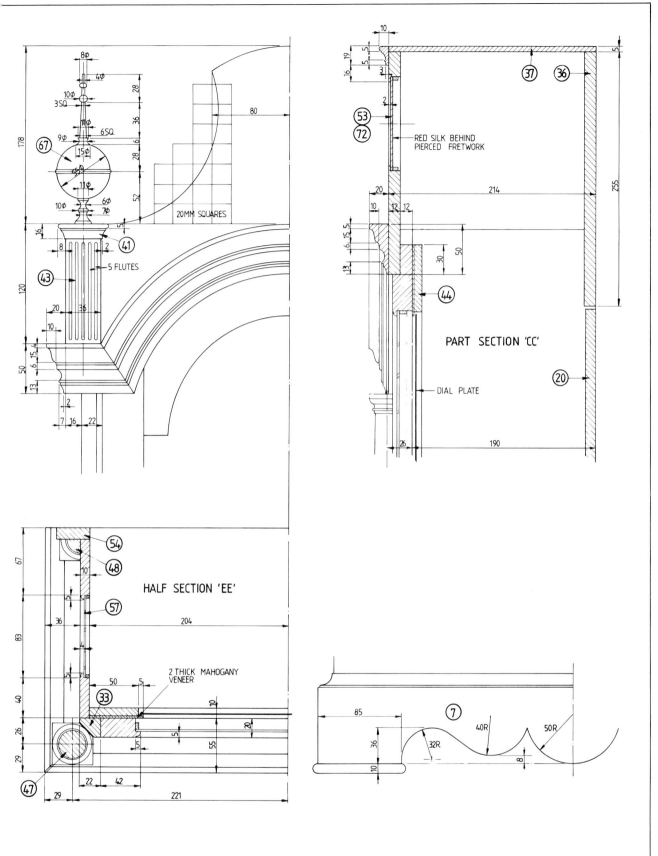

PART SECTION 'CC'

RED SILK BEHIND
PIERCED FRETWORK

DIAL PLATE

5 FLUTES

20MM SQUARES

HALF SECTION 'EE'

2 THICK MAHOGANY
VENEER

17.9 *Hood sections and plinth arrangement*

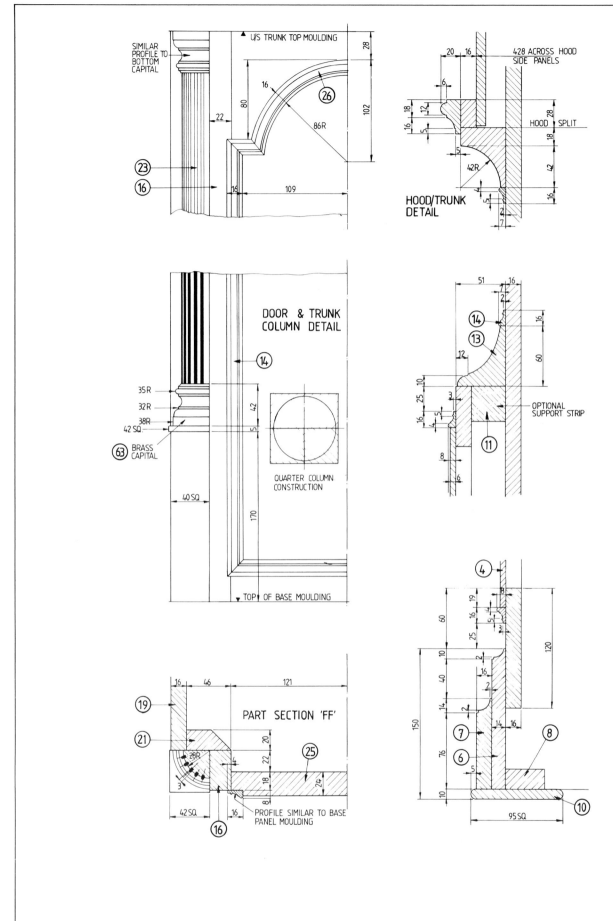

17.10 *Trunk and moulding details*

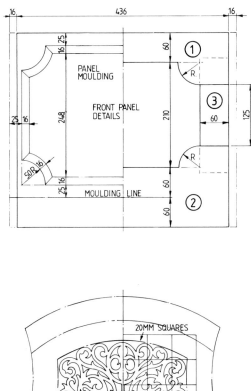

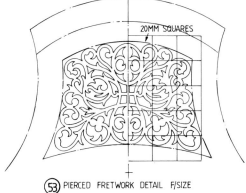

(53) PIERCED FRETWORK DETAIL F/SIZE

17.11 *Base framework and hood fret pattern*

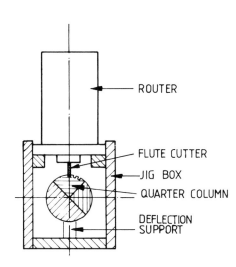

JIG GUIDE BOX

17.12 *Jig guide box*

the original clock had doors fitted with period brass pattern escutcheons it was usual only to fit small brass key pipes on this type of clock.

Movement

Fit an eight day weight driven movement striking on a bell and with a seconds pendulum. Post this to a 305mm (12in) arch dial plate. These are more commonly available sized 280mm (11in) so you may have to do some hunting around to acquire this item. However, they can be made up individually to suit and this may offer a solution. There is another more radical alternative which is to adapt the design to suit the smaller 280mm (11in) dial by proportionally reducing the casework to suit.

PARTS LIST

Item	No	Material	Dimensions (mm)
Base			
1 Front panel top rail	1	Mahogany	105×16×432 long
2 Front panel bottom rail	1	Mahogany	165×16×432 long
3 Front panel side rail	2	Mahogany	60×16×230 long
4 Base centre panel	1	Mahogany	248×6×386 long
5 Side panel	2	Mahogany	230×16×395 long
6 Plinth rail (1)	1	Mahogany	140×14×1020 long total
7 Plinth rail (2)	4	Mahogany	90×16×1070 long total
8 Corner pad	4	Mahogany	40×20×40 long
9 Fillet strip	1	Mahogany	15sq×400 long. Fit in short strips
10 Foot pad	4	Mahogany	95×10×400 long total. Cut into four pieces
11 Trunk support strip	1	Mahogany	35sq×900 long total. Optional fitting

12	Back strip	2	Mahogany	35×10×435 long
13	Base moulding (1)	1	Mahogany	60×51×950 long total
14	Edge moulding (2)	1	Mahogany	16×8×4650 long total requirement for all case
15	Corner moulding (3)	1	Mahogany	150×8×150 long total. Split into four after maching

Trunk

16	Stile	2	Mahogany	40×22×1370 long
17	Cross rail (1)	1	Mahogany	188×16×286 long
18	Cross rail (2)	1	Mahogany	200×16×286 long
19	Trunk side	2	Mahogany	128×16×1370 long
20	Back board	1	Oak	366×10×2120 long
21	Trunk support strip	2	Mahogany	46×20×1370 long
22	Trunk corner block	2	Mahogany	40sq×570 long. Split in two pieces
23	Quarter column	2	Mahogany	35sq×740 long
24	Column pad piece	2	Mahogany	42×5×42 long
25	Trunk door panel	1	Mahogany	242×24×939 long
26	Door arch moulding (4)	1	Mahogany	100×8×220 long
27	Trunk top moulding (5)	1	Mahogany	60×47×940 long total
28	Seat board	1	Oak	168×18×366 long

Hood

| 29 | Front rail | 1 | Mahogany | 35×28×460 long |
| 30 | Side rail | 2 | Mahogany | 16×28×225 long |

31	Rail edge moulding (6)	1	Mahogany	34×20×1020 long total
32	Hood side panel	2	Mahogany	190×10×576 long
33	Hood door architrave	2	Mahogany	22×20×384 long
34	Pagoda arch panel	1	Mahogany	343×12×428 long
35	Inner arch panel	1	Mahogany	170×12×428 long
36	Rear arch panel	1	Oak	255×12×428 long
37	Hood roof segment	30	Pine	25×5×214 long. Bend to suit. Fit in strips
38	Hood side strip	2	Mahogany	165×16×214 long
39	Hood arch moulding (7)	1	Mahogany	172×20×420 long
40	Hood moulding (8)	2	Mahogany	50×20×450 long
41	Hood moulding (9)	1	Mahogany	16×8×600 long
42	Pagoda arch moulding (10)	1	Mahogany	55×10×180 long
43	Pagoda flute strip	2	Mahogany	36×10×104 long
44	Mask arch panel	1	Pine	200×8×408 long
45	Mask side strip	2	Pine	50×8×420 long
46	Mask bottom strip	1	Pine	68×8×408 long
47	Front pillar	2	Mahogany	40sq×410 long, see notes
48	Quarter pillar	2	Mahogany	20sq×410 long, see notes
49	Door frame (arch)	1	Mahogany	170×20×384 long
50	Door frame (side)	2	Mahogany	42×20×420 long
51	Door frame (bottom)	1	Mahogany	42×20×384 long
52	Beading	1	Mahogany	5×3×1050 long total
53	Fretwork panel	1	Mahogany	100×2.5×150 long
54	Splat strip	2	Mahogany	35×12×384 long

55	Veneer	–	Mahogany	Quantity to suit trunk door & base front panel

Glass

56	Door glass	1	Picture glass	Cut to fit hood door
57	Sidelight glass	2	Picture glass	230×83 approx

Metalwork components

58	Trunk door hinge	2	Brass	Longcase pattern
59	Trunk door lock	1	Brass	Purchase to suit
60	Escutcheon (pipe)	2	Brass	Purchase to suit
61	Hood door hinge	2	Brass	25 long×16 wide
62	Hood door lock	1	Brass	Purchase to suit
63	Trunk column capital	4	Brass	Purchase to suit
64	Brass reed (1)	10	Brass	5×3×225 long
65	Hood column capital	4	Brass	Purchase to suit
66	Brass reed (2)	12	Brass	3×2×112 long
67	Ball & spire finial	2	Brass	Purchase to suit

Movement & dial

68	Dial plate/ spandrels	1	Brass	305sq nominal size c/w moonphase segment
69	Chapter ring	1	–	To suit dial plate
70	Movement/ pendulum	1	–	Eight day striking on bell c/w seconds to pendulum
71	Minute/ hour hand	1 set	–	Purchase to suit
72	Silk cloth	1	Red silk	To fit behind pierced fretwork

CHAPTER 18

Swan neck longcase clock (c. 1810)

In the second half of the eighteenth century another style of longcase clock was introduced which had a hood with a so called 'swan neck' pediment (Fig 18.1). As its name suggests it is an undulating ogee shape finishing with a rounded end, and the shape mimics that of the bird's neck. The pediment gives the appearance of two swans facing one another. The beginnings of the swan neck feature can often be noted in carved pediments adorning furniture and clocks of earlier date. In a Tompion longcase I saw recently the ogee outline and rosette end were clearly visible in the carved crestwork. The swan neck hood is best suited to the arch dial though sometimes one is fitted to a round dial plate.

Another aspect that can be noted in this longcase design is the general trend towards larger dial plates. The very earliest dial plates c.1660 were 200mm (8in) square, but within ten years quickly changed to 250mm (10in) (e.g. marquetry clock Chapter 15). In the early part of the eighteenth century the dial size increased to 280mm (11in), and in the larger clocks, e.g. London pagoda, advanced to 300mm (12in). In the 1770s the dial plate was made even larger up to 340mm square (13½in). This could still be fitted into a standard hood width of around 390mm (15½in) designed to accommodate a normal 280mm brass dial plate, but the hood door width was made narrower to suit the larger minute ring which was often 300–330mm (12–13in) diameter.

Case description

This design is measured from a Lancashire longcase clock c.1775, and the principal case features are as follows. The hood accommodates a large arched dial with a swan neck pediment above and simple turned pillars to the side. There is a brass eagle/ball finial in the centre. Below this is a trunk which has a narrow twin spire top door with quarter columns either side and ring turned capitals. Of particular note is the Chippendale style fret below the trunk top moulding, a simple attractive feature which the casemaker subtly incorporated to improve the appearance. The base is of the framed type and the case stands on small ogee feet. The arch dial plate is nominally 343mm square (13½in) with a silvered chapter ring marked with Roman and Arabic numerals and has a centre sweep seconds hand. Above this is a moon/tidal phase crescent. There are 'questionmark' pattern spandrels in the corners and the dial is signed 'Simpson, Wigton'. The movement is eight day striking on a bell.

Construction

The general arrangement is given in Fig 18.4 and principal sections in Fig 18.5. Sections through the case at various levels and the hood layout is shown in Figs 18.6 and 18.7. More detailed aspects of the hood and mouldings etc are given in Fig 18.8.

Trunk

The trunk box is a box construction consisting of a door framework, quarter columns, sides and back. Butt joint the sides and back, and connect the door framework items using mortice and tenons. Strengthen the trunk internally with softwood fillet as necessary. Construct the

18.1 *Swan neck longcase clock*

18.2 *Simpson Wigton dial plate*

18.3 *Trunk fretwork detail*

143

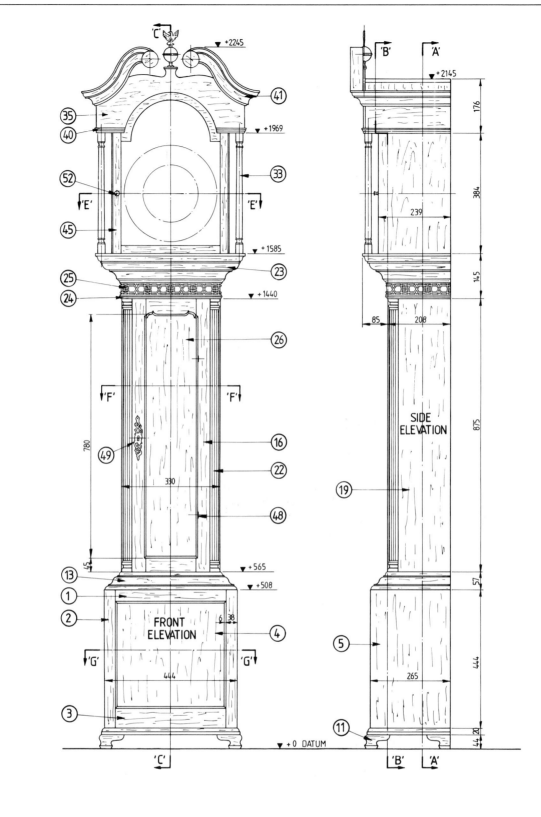

18.4 *General arrangement of swan neck longcase clock*

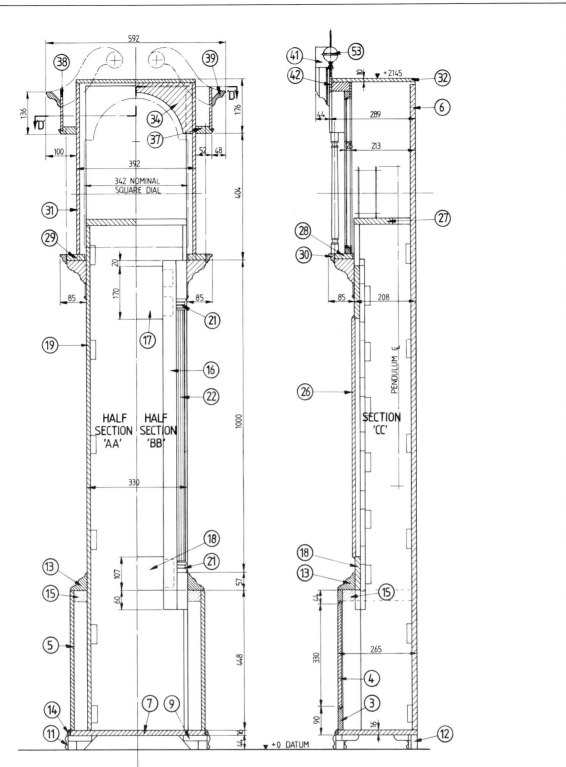

18.5 *Sectional arrangement of swan neck longcase clock*

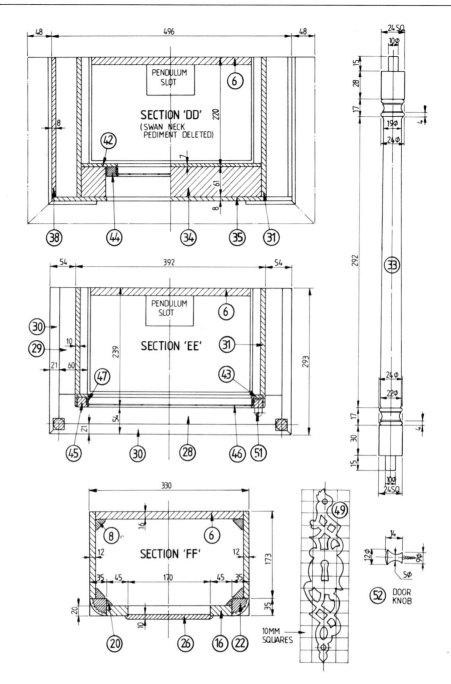

18.6 *Cross sections through casework*

quarter columns similar to those on the pagoda clock (Chapter 17). On this case the quarter capitals extend the full trunk height, and the capitals are woodturned rather than brass.

Base

The base design on this longcase clock uses the more stable framed construction for the front panel comprising rails (1), (2) and (3) jointed by mortice and tenons. Groove these rails internally

to suit the middle panel (4). Otherwise make the base similar to the Lancashire longcase clock (Chapter 16). In the original the trunk sides are carried through to the bottom but this is optional.

Hood

The hood is a square box with the swan neck pediment applied to the front. In many respects it is similar to the Lancashire clock excepting for

Hood fretwork

I have mentioned earlier the application of Chippendale fretwork to the top of the trunk, and it is worth mentioning that the swan neck longcase clock in particular lends itself to the addition of fretwork on the hood. Blind fretwork is often incorporated on the panel above the hood door arch, and sometimes pierced fretwork is fitted in the space between the swan neck pediment arches. These are alternatives both worth considering.

Movement and dial

Finding a suitable brass dial plate to fit to this clock may pose problems mainly because of its size, but there is no reason why you should not make it up from individual components. An alternative solution is to consider fitting a standard 280mm (11in) brass dial plate/chapter ring arrangement. If you do this you will need to widen the hood door framework similar to the Lancashire longcase clock. Fit an eight day weight driven movement with a seconds pendulum preferably striking on a bell.

Trunk and base – construction summary

At the conclusion of this design I want to summarize four important aspects of longcase clock design seen in earlier chapters. These are the construction of trunk framework, trunk door design, trunk door profiles and base design.

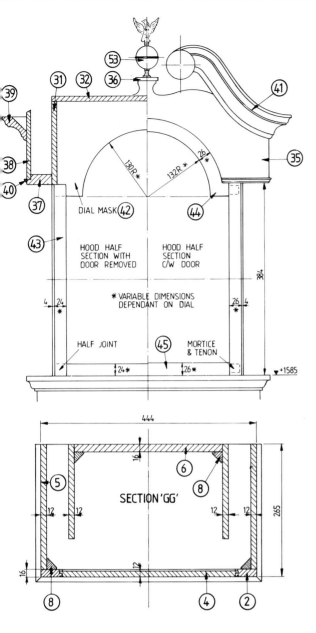

18.7 *Hood layout and section 'GG'*

Trunk frames

There are in principle three types of trunk framework used on longcase clocks as illustrated in Fig 18.9. In the first the top and bottom rails extend across the full width of the trunk and are half jointed over the stiles as in (A). This construction is used mainly on veneered and japanned casework, and situations where the horizontal joint is subsequently covered. An example of this framework design is the marquetry longcase clock (Chapter 15). In the second type of frame (B) the top and bottom rails are either mortice and tenoned into the

the arch dial section, with the hood sides morticed into the support rails, a half jointed mask framework rebated into the sides and a side soffit detail. A suggestion to make the hood assembly easier is to extend the bottom section of the mask over the back face of the front support rail (28). The hood door is a standard half jointed assembly hinged on plates top and bottom. The most testing part of the hood construction is the swan neck pediment. This is set out on a squared background in Fig 18.8 to aid transfer of the pattern to the wood.

147

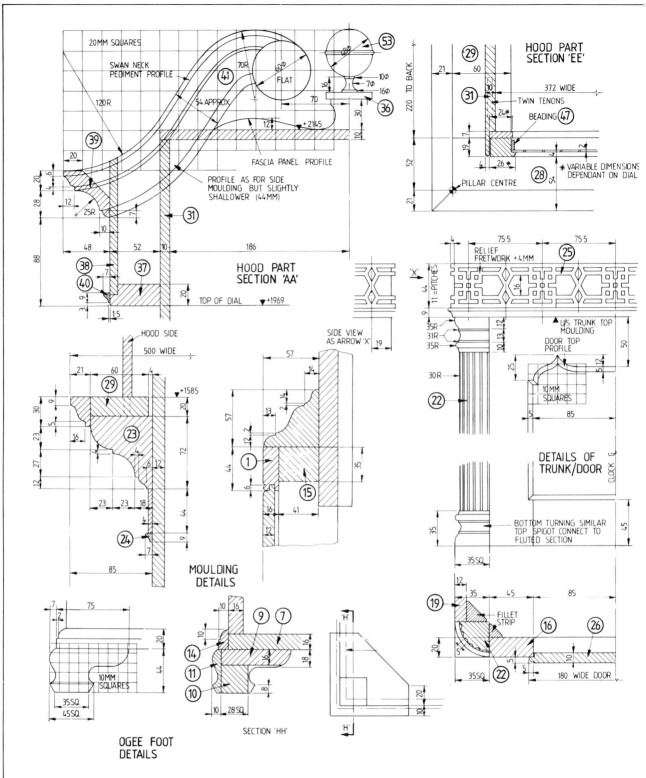

18.8 *Hood sections and trunk details*

stiles or alternatively half jointed behind. This is used mainly on solid hardwood casework and situations where it is undesirable to see a visible horizontal joint. In general terms this applies to post 1750 casework. Examples of this are the Lancashire and pagoda longcase clock designs (Chapters 16 and 17). Occasionally one sees a mitred corner trunk frame construction (C) but from a woodworking aspect this is more difficult to make accurately, and I have purposely avoided designs with this type of frame. It should be noted that the above generalisation is by no means a rigid rule and the final choice is very much case dependent.

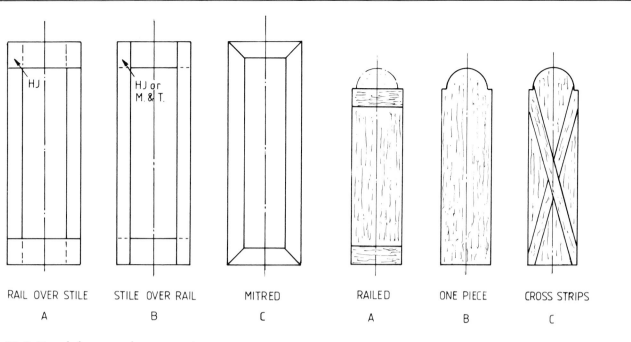

RAIL OVER STILE
A

STILE OVER RAIL
B

MITRED
C

18.9 *Trunk framework construction*

RAILED
A

ONE PIECE
B

CROSS STRIPS
C

18.10 *Trunk door construction*

18.11 *Trunk door veneer crazing*

Trunk doors

There are two principal trunk door types as shown in Fig 18.10. In the first the door consists of a centre board with a transverse strip laid either end (A), and the second uses a one piece construction as in (B). The three part construction seems to be an attempt to minimize warping and reduce visible end grain, but often the connection is only a plain butt joint. Obviously there is scope at least for inserting a loose tongue strip between them to stiffen the arrangement. If the door is veneered externally using the type (A) construction this sometimes leads to cracks appearing later at the joint due to

wood movement (Fig 18.11). If a one piece door construction is proposed warping can be minimized by selecting quarter sawn timber. One rather sophisticated solution to the problem of warping that I spotted on a Bristol longcase clock was to insert two cross strips let into the surface of the door as in (C).

Trunk door styles

The preceding longcase clock designs show trunk doors with four of the most common trunk shapes. These are the flat top, wavy top, broken arch round top, and the spired top. However there are one hundred and one variations and Fig 18.12 shows some of the more common styles divided into four categories, flat, wavy, domed and spired.

The earliest longcase clocks had flat top doors as in (A) (e.g. marquetry clock Chapter 15) and this predominated up until about 1700. After this date case makers became more experimental and trunk door shapes often reflected a hood feature because it made an aesthetically pleasing combination. Fig 18.12 (B), (C) and (D) shows some variations of flat tops with the addition of simple curved corner features. Style (B) for example could have been for a trunk which had a parquetry fan motif feature in the corner, and

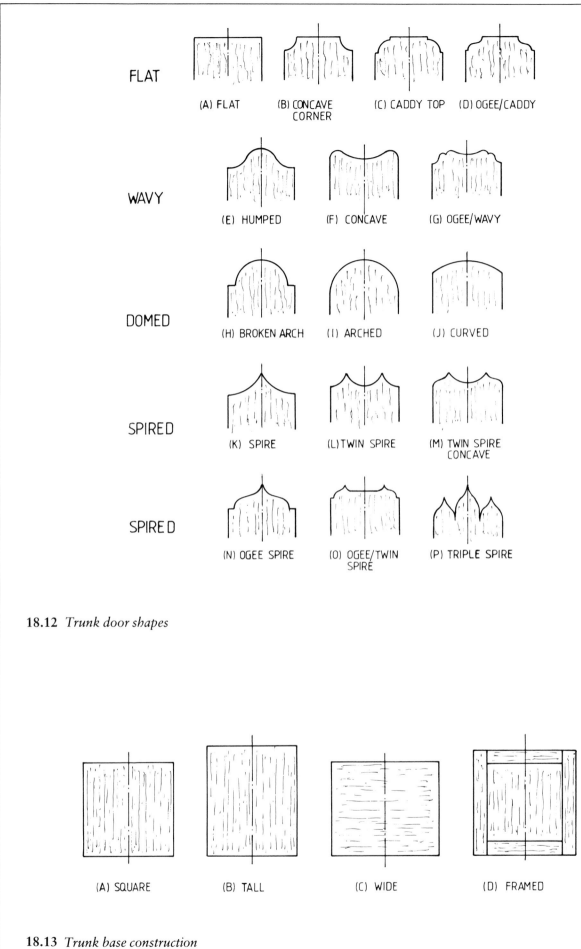

FLAT

(A) FLAT　　(B) CONCAVE CORNER　　(C) CADDY TOP　　(D) OGEE/CADDY

WAVY

(E) HUMPED　　(F) CONCAVE　　(G) OGEE/WAVY

DOMED

(H) BROKEN ARCH　　(I) ARCHED　　(J) CURVED

SPIRED

(K) SPIRE　　(L) TWIN SPIRE　　(M) TWIN SPIRE CONCAVE

SPIRED

(N) OGEE SPIRE　　(O) OGEE/TWIN SPIRE　　(P) TRIPLE SPIRE

18.12 *Trunk door shapes*

(A) SQUARE　　(B) TALL　　(C) WIDE　　(D) FRAMED

18.13 *Trunk base construction*

styles (C) and (D) might have been used in combination with cases with caddy top hoods. Characteristic wavy top shapes are shown in (E), (F) and (G). The wavy top/ogee corner style (G) was a very popular pattern used over a long period of time. Dome top styles as in (H), (I) and (J) tended to get used on clocks which had hoods with similar features, and (H) in particular was used on broken arch and pagoda style hoods. Spire top doors came mainly in single and twin spire variants combined with ogees, and you sometimes find these married to hoods with swan neck pediments. You do also find styles (E) and (G) linked with the swan neck feature. Having said all this you do sometimes find the strangest combinations, and the above should be treated only as a guide to promote good aesthetic casework design.

Bases

The study of base design of period longcase clocks reveals nothing special or complicated. In the plain panel type of construction the basic rule is to make the grain go in the direction of the longest edge as illustrated in Fig 18.13. Thus if the panel is square or tall the grain is always vertical as in (A) and (B), but a panel which is wider than the height should be laid with the grain horizontal as in (C). In many ways trunk bases are similar to early seventeenth century plank chests with long and cross grain timber joined together, a combination which has no regard for wood movement, and try as you may you will usually find some item where the glued parts are pulling against one another. The potential for stress cracks appearing on trunk bases under varying humidity conditions is hence high unless due consideration is given to minimizing this.

One method of minimizing wood movement is to use quarter sawn timber because this moves about half that of wood sawn through-and-through. It is also much less likely to warp and in the case of oak has an interesting ray fleck pattern.

Another solution is to use the framed construction as in Fig 18.13 (D), where the centre panel is fitted in grooves and is free to move. A third solution is to use modern alternatives such as plywood or blockboard which do offer a much more stable construction, but whether you use these depends on how authentic the clock case is to be. If they are used a veneered finish will usually be necessary.

PARTS LIST

Item	No	Material	Dimensions (mm)
Base			
1 Base top rail	1	Oak	44×16×444 long
2 Base side rail	2	Oak	44×16×444 long
3 Base bottom rail	1	Oak	74×16×444 long
4 Base centre panel	1	Oak	386×12×338 long
5 Base side	2	Oak	249×12×448 long
6 Back board	1	Pine	306×16×2070 long
7 Bottom	1	Pine	265×16×444 long
8 Corner fillet (1)	1	Pine	15sq×1800 long. Total required for all case
9 Support pad	4	Beech	72×16×72 long
10 Support block	4	Beech	28sq×28 long
11 Ogee foot moulding	6	Oak	44×10×85 long
12 Back foot support	2	Oak	44×20×100 long

13	Base top moulding	1	Oak	57sq×100 long total
14	Base edge moulding	1	Oak	20×10×1030 long total
15	Trunk support strip	1	Oak	41×35×820 long total. Optional fitting

Trunk

16	Stile	2	Oak	45×20×1117 long
17	Cross rail (1)	1	Oak	170×20×250 long
18	Cross rail (2)	1	Oak	167×20×260 long
19	Trunk side	2	Oak	173×12×1600 long
20	Corner fillet (2)	2	Oak	15sq×1600 long
21	Column end piece	4	Oak	35sq×170 long
22	Reeded quarter column	2	Oak	30sq×830 long
23	Trunk top moulding (1)	1	Oak	85×72×1090 long total
24	Trunk top moulding (2)	1	Oak	9×7×800 long total
25	Chinese fretwork	2	Oak	44×4×780 long
26	Door	1	Oak	180×10×800 long
27	Seat board	1	Oak	192×20×330 long

Hood

28	Front support rail (1)	1	Oak	52×20×458 long
29	Side support rail (2)	2	Oak	60×20×272 long
30	Rail edge moulding	1	Oak	30×21×1100 long total
31	Hood side panel	2	Oak	281×10×570 long
32	Roof board	1	Oak	281×10×392 long
33	Pillar	2	Oak	24sq×415 long
34	Crest panel	1	Oak	166×61×372 long

35	Crest fascia	1	Oak	188×8×490 long
36	Finial support strip	1	Oak	16×7×48 long
37	Side soffit	2	Oak	52×20×281 long
38	Side fascia	2	Oak	140×8×281 long
39	Hood moulding (1)	2	Oak	70×20×335 long
40	Hood moulding (2)	1	Oak	9×7×850 long total
41	Swan neck pediment	2	Oak	90×44×300 long
42	Mask pediment panel	1	Oak	190×7×384 long
43	Mask side/bottom strip	2	Oak	24×7×384 long
44	Hood door frame (arch)	1	Oak	158×19×384 long
45	Hood door frame (sides/bottom)	3	Oak	26×19×384 long
46	Glass pane	1	Picture glass	To fit hood door
47	Beading	3	Oak	10×4×345 long

Metalwork components

48	Trunk door hinge	2	Brass	Longcase pattern
49	Escutcheon	1	Brass	Purchase to suit
50	Lock	1	Brass	Purchase to suit
51	Hood door pivot	2	Brass	15×30 strip screw fixed
52	Door knob	1	Brass	12 nominal dia. Purchase to suit
53	Eagle ball finial	1	Brass	Purchase to suit

Movement & dial

54	Dial/spandrels	1	Brass	342sq nominal c/w moonphase crescent
55	Movement/pendulum	1	–	Eight day striking on bell c/w seconds pendulum
56	Minute/hour hand	1 pr	–	

Glossary

Arbor: A term used to describe an axle used to carry gears or pinions etc.

Anchor escapement: Consists of a curved metal anchor with pallet ends engaging with a toothed escape wheel beneath. The rocking motion of the anchor unlocks the escape wheel a tooth at a time to regulate the escape of power from the movement.

Balance wheel: An oscillating rimmed wheel controlling the rate at which a movement unwinds.

Barrel: The cylindrical housing mounted on the winding arbor to which the weight line is attached. In winding up the weight line is wrapped around the outside of the barrel. On a spring driven clock the barrel contains a spring within.

Birdcage: The framework of a movement consisting of a pair of horizontal plates joined together by vertical pillars or posts. Usually used in the context of longcase clocks.

Bob: The heavy weight on the end of the pendulum.

Chapter ring: The silvered ring applied to the front of a dial plate and marked with Roman and/or Arabic numerals and the minute ring.

Cock plate: The bracket used to support the pendulum, fixed either to the top of the movement or in the case of Vienna regulators the back of the case.

Crown wheel: A toothed wheel mounted on a vertical arbor. Used in the context of verge escapements.

Crutch: A metal connecting device to link the pendulum to the escapement.

Dead beat escapement: A precision escapement used on high quality clocks which does not have any recoil.

Pillars: Used to connect the front and back plates of a movement.

False plate: A false plate is sometimes interposed between the movement and the dial plate where it is not easy to connect the two directly together.

Fusee: A chain or gut arrangement at one end connected to the barrel and at the other wrapped around a fusee (step shaped) pulley. Used on spring driven clocks to equalize the torque applied to the movement during unwinding.

Foliot: An early form of balance wheel consisting of an oscillating arm with adjustable weights on either side.

Lenticule: A glazed round or oval opening in the trunk door of a longcase clock.

Maintaining power: A mechanism to keep a clock working so that it does not lose time whilst it is being rewound.

Motion work: The 12:1 gear reduction used to drive the hour hand slower than the minute hand.

Pallet: The spade like end pieces on a verge, anchor or dead beat escapement used to lock the escape wheel.

Pendulum: Consists of a rod with a heavy bob used to regulate the time keeping of a clock. The period of oscillation depends on gravity and the pendulum length.

Rating nut: The screw at the bottom of a pendulum used to raise and lower the heavy metal bob and adjust the timing of a clock.

Spandrel: A decorative brass casting used to fill the corner spaces on square dial clocks external to the chapter ring.

Verge: An early form of escapement using a crown wheel and pallet arrangement.

METRIC/IMPERIAL CONVERSION TABLE

Millimetres	Inches	Millimetres	Inches	Millimetres	Inches	Millimetres	Inches
1.5	1/16″	25	1″	125	4 15/16″	900	35 7/8″
3	1/8″	30	1 3/16″	150	5 7/8″	1000	39 3/8″
5	3/16″	35	1 3/8″	200	7 7/8″	1500	59 1/8″
6	1/4″	38	1 1/2″	300	11 13/16″	2000	78 3/4″
8	5/16″	40	1 9/16″	305	12″	2500	98 7/16″
10	3/8″	45	1 3/4″	400	15 3/4″	3000	118 1/8″
13	1/2″	50	2″	500	19 11/16″	3500	137 3/4″
16	5/8″	60	2 3/8″	600	23 5/8″	4000	157 1/2″
19	3/4″	75	3″	700	27 9/16″	4500	177 1/8″
22	7/8″	100	3 15/16″	800	31 1/2″	5000	196 7/8″

Pendulum vibration

The period of oscillation of a simple pendulum from side to side is:

$$T = \pi\sqrt{L/G} \quad \text{where}$$

T = period of oscillation (seconds)
L = length of pendulum (metres)
G = acceleration due to gravity (nominally 9.811 metres/sec)
π = 3.142

The lengths of pendulums for periods of oscillation commonly available are:

½ second   249mm
¾ second   559mm
1 second   994mm

The pendulum length is from the theoretical point of suspension to the centre of the bob assuming the pendulum rod is weightless. A pendulum is usually supported from a cock plate through a small piece of flat spring steel. Due to the flexure of this the theoretical point of suspension is actually slightly below the actual suspension point. The period of oscillation also depends on the value of the acceleration due to gravity which varies slightly in different parts of the world.

Clock Museums

American Clock and Watch Museum
100 Maple Street
Bristol, CT
(203) 583–6070

Henry Francis DuPont Winterthur Museum
Winterthur, DE
(302) 656–8591 or 1–800–448–3883

Smithsonian Institute
National Museum of American History
Washington, D.C.
(202) 357–1300

Time Museum
7801 E. State Street
Rockford, IL
(815) 398–6000

The Bily Clock Exhibit Horology Museum
Spillville, IA
(319) 562–3569

Old Sturbridge Village
Sturbridge, MA
(617) 347–3362

Willard House
Grafton, MA
(617) 839–3500

Henry Ford Museum/Greenfield Village
Dearborne, MI
(313) 271–1620

Metropolitan Museum of Art
5th Avenue and 82nd Street
New York, NY
(212) 535–7710

Hoffman Foundation
Newark Public Library
Newark, NY
(315) 331–4370

Old Salem, Inc.
614 Main Street
Winston–Salem, NC
(919) 723–3688

Museum of the American Watchmakers Institute
3700 Harrison Avenue
Cincinnati, OH
(513) 661–3838

National Museum of Clocks and Watches
514 Poplar Street
Columbia, PA
(717) 684–8261

Old Clock Museum
929 East Preston
Pharr, TX
(512) 787–1923

Suppliers

Beveled Glass

Beveled Glass Works
611 North Tillamook
Portland, OR 97227

Paint

Cohassett Colonials
Cohassett, MA 02025

Stulb Paint and Chemical Co. Inc.
P.O. Box 297
Norristown, PA 19404

Stains/Tung Oil

Cohassett Colonials
Cohassett, MA 02025

Deft Inc.
17451 Von Darman Avenue
Irvine, CA 92713-9507

Formby's Inc.
825 Crossover Lane, Suite 240
Memphis, TN 38117

Stulb Paint and Chemical Co. Inc.
P.O. Box 297
Norristown, PA 19404

Watco-Dennis Corp.
Michigan Avenue & 22nd Street
Santa Monica, CA 90404

Old-Fashioned Nails/Screws

Equality Screw Co. Inc.
P.O. Box 1645
El Cajon, CA 92022

Horton Brasses
P.O. Box 120-K
Nooks Hill Road
Cromwell, CT 06416

Tremont Nail Co.
P.O. Box 111
21 Elm Street
Wareham, MA 02571

Brasses

Anglo-American Brass Co.
P.O. Box 9792
4146 Mitzi Drive
San Jose, CA 95157–0792

Ball and Ball
463 West Lincoln Highway
Exton, PA 19341

The Brass Tree
308 North Main Street
Charles, MO 63301

Garrett Wade Co. Inc.
161 Avenue of the Americas
New York, NY 10013

Heirloom Antiques Brass Co.
P.O. Box 146
Dundass, MN 55019

Horton Brasses
P.O. Box 120-K
Nooks Hill Road
Cromwell, CT 06416

Imported European Hardware
4295 South Arville
Las Vegas, NV 89103

19th Century Co. Hardware Supply Co.
P.O. Box 599
Rough and Ready, CA 95975

The Renovator's Supply
Millers Falls, MA 01349

The Shop, Inc.
P.O. Box 3711, R.D. 3
Reading, PA 19606

Ritter and Son Hardware
Dept. WJ
Gualala, CA 95445

Veneering

Bob Morgan Woodworking Supplies
1123 Bardstown Road
Louisville, KY 40204

General Catalogs

Brookstone Co.
Vose Farm Road
Peterborough, NH 03458

Constantine
2050 Eastchester Road
Bronx, NY 10461

Cryder Creek Wood Shoppe, Inc.
P.O. Box 19
Whitesville, NY 14897

The Fine Tool Shops
P.O. Box 1262
20 Backus Avenue
Danbury, CT 06810

Leichtung Inc.
4944 Commerce Parkway
Cleveland, OH 44128

Silvo Hardware Co.
2205 Richmond Street
Philadelphia, PA 19125

Trendlines
375 Beacham Street
Chelsea, MA 02150

Woodcraft Supply
7845 Emerson Avenue
Parkersburg, WV 26102

The Woodworker's Store
21801 Industrial Boulevard
Rogers, MN 55374

Woodworkers Supply of New Mexico
5604 Alameda, N.E.
Albuquerque, NM 87113

Movements

Armor Products
P.O. Box 445
East Northport, NY 11731

Barap Specialties
835 Bellows Avenue
Frankfort, MI 49635

Craft Products Co.
2200 Dean Street
St. Charles, IL 60176

Craftsman Wood Service Company
1735 West Cortland Court
Addison, IL 60101

Emperor Clock Company
Emperor Industrial Park
Fairhope, AL 36532

Innovation Specialties
11869 Teale St.
Culver City, CA 90230

International Clock Craft Ltd.
52 Isabel Street
Winnipeg, Manitoba, Canada

Kidder Klock Company
39-3 Glen Cameron Road #3
Thornhill, Ontario, Canada

Klockit
P.O. Box 542
N3211 Highway H North
Lake Geneva, WI 53147-9961

Kuempel Chime Clockworks and Studio, Inc.
21195 Minnetonka Boulevard
Excelsior, MN 55331

Mason and Sullivan (now Woodcraft Supply Corp.)
7845 Emerson Avenue
Parkersburg, WV 26102

Merritt Antiques Inc.
P.O. Box 277
Douglassville, PA 19518

M.L. Shipley and Co.
Rt. 2, Box 161
Cassville, MO 65625

Murray Clock Craft Limited
510 McNicoll Avenue
Willowdale, Ontario, Canada

National Artcraft Company
23456 Mercantile Road
Beachwood, OH 44122

Newport Enterprises, Inc.
2313 West Burbank Boulevard
Burbank, CA 91506

Pacific Time Company
138 West 7th Street
Eureka, CA 95501

Precision Movements
P.O. Box 689
2024 Chestnut Street
Emmaus, PA 18049

Selva Borel
347 13th Street
Oakland, CA 94604

S. LaRose Inc.
234 Commerce Place
Greensboro, NC 27420

Southwest Clock Supply Inc.
2442 Walnut Ridge
Dallas, TX 75229

T. E. C. Specialties
P.O. Box 909
Smyrna, GA 30081

Viking Clock Co.
Foley Industrial Park
P.O. Box 490
Foley, AL 36536

Westwood Clock 'N Kits
2850-B East 29th Street
Long Beach, CA 90806

Reverse Glass and Dial Painting

Astrid C. Donnellan
21 Mast Hill Road
Hingham, MA 02043

Marianne Picazio
P.O. Box 1523
Buzzard's Bay, MA 02532

Linda Rivard
27 Spur Lane,
Newington, CT 06111

Linda Abrams
26 Chestnut Avenue
Burlington, MA 01803

Judith W. Akey
173 Penn Harb Road
Pennington, NJ 08534

The Shipley Company
2075 South University Boulevard #199
Denver, CO 80210

Special Custom Wood Turnings

Boland V. Tapp Imports
13525 Alondra Boulevard
Santa Fe Springs, CA 90670

River Bend Turnings
Box 364
RD1
Wellsville, NY 14689

Wooden Needle
Box 908
Kamloops, B.C., Canada

Index